ISLAM AND WORLD HISTORY

JAMES A. MILLWARD, SERIES EDITOR

The Silk Roads series is made possible by the generous support of the Henry Luce Foundation's Asia Program. Founded in 1936, the Luce Foundation is a not-for-profit philanthropic organization devoted to promoting innovation in academic, policy, religious, and art communities. The Asia Program aims to foster cultural and intellectual exchange between the United States and the countries of East and Southeast Asia, and to create scholarly and public resources for improved understanding of Asia in the United States.

ALSO IN THE SERIES:

Sacred Mandates: Asian International Relations since Chinggis Khan
Edited by Timothy Brook, Michael van Walt van Praag, and Miek Boltjes
Published 2018

ISLAM
AND
World History

The Ventures of Marshall Hodgson

EDITED BY

Edmund Burke III

and

Robert J. Mankin

THE UNIVERSITY OF CHICAGO PRESS

CHICAGO AND LONDON

This book was published with the generous support of the University of Chicago Center in Paris. The center aims to develop intellectual and academic exchanges between France and the United States, offering classes in all disciplines; a research institute for graduate students, postdoctoral scholars, and professors from the University of Chicago whose work focuses on French culture and civilization; and debates, conferences, and colloquia aimed at facilitating and promoting academic collaboration between American and European researchers, as well as Paris-based alumni.

The University of Chicago Press, Chicago 60637
The University of Chicago Press, Ltd., London

Published 2018
Printed in the United States of America

27 26 25 24 23 22 21 20 19 18   1 2 3 4 5

ISBN-13: 978-0-226-58464-5 (cloth)
ISBN-13: 978-0-226-58478-2 (paper)
ISBN-13: 978-0-226-58481-2 (e-book)
DOI: https://doi.org/10.7208/chicago/9780226584812.001.0001

Library of Congress Cataloging-in-Publication Data

Names: Burke, Edmund, 1940– editor. | Mankin, Robert, editor.
Title: Islam and world history : the ventures of Marshall Hodgson / edited by Edmund Burke III and Robert J. Mankin.
Other titles: Silk roads (Chicago, Ill.)
Description: Chicago ; London : The University of Chicago Press, 2018. | Series: Silk roads | Includes bibliographical references.
Identifiers: LCCN 2018022270 | ISBN 9780226584645 (cloth : alk. paper) | ISBN 9780226584782 (pbk. : alk. paper) | ISBN 9780226584812 (e-book)
Subjects: LCSH: Hodgson, Marshall G. S. | Islamic countries—History.
Classification: LCC DS35.63 .I648 2018 | DDC 909/.09767—dc23
LC record available at https://lccn.loc.gov/2018022270

♾ This paper meets the requirements of ANSI/NISO Z39.48-1992 (Permanence of Paper).

CONTENTS

Hodgson and the New Islamic Studies

CHAPTER ONE

The Ventures of Marshall G. S. Hodgson

Edmund Burke III and Robert J. Mankin

How far over the curve of the horizon to the future is it possible to see?

Marshall Hodgson and His Many Legacies

To engage with Hodgson's thought is to apprehend the world of Islam through different spectacles. When it appeared in 1974, Hodgson's *The Venture of Islam: Conscience and History in a World Civilization* was recognized as a major achievement.[1] For the first time an American historian cast Islam in a world-historical frame and simultaneously asserted its moral vision. In doing so, Hodgson proposed a radical response to the persistent cultural biases that had stunted the growth of the Islamic studies field. For him Islam was not "other"; it was a venture alongside others that marked human efforts to bring about a just and moral world.

At present, the very idea of Islam as a monotheistic religion with a moral vision is impossible for most people to imagine. So too is the thought that the history of Islamic civilization is primarily the history of the Arabs. (In fact, fully 80 percent of world Muslims do not speak Arabic.) Although many people are aware that not all Muslims are Sunni, few know that 10–13 percent are adherents of the Shiʿa branch. Hodgson believed that rather than being of little consequence, these internal differences played a vital role in shaping how Islamic civilization unfolded.

This had several consequences for Hodgson. First, to "get Islam right," it was necessary to rethink its place in the larger context of human history. Far from having an autonomous history, Islamic civilization is deeply embedded in the history of the rest of human society. Second, there would need to be a fundamental rethinking of the concept of civilization. Civilizations for Hodgson were not autonomous, culturally defined, and changeless spaces. Rather, they had had historically complex and often conflicting relationships internally as well as with their neighbors.

Changing our conception of civilization meant reinventing world history as well. Hodgson also had to reshape the field of world history. His world history began with the notion of the interconnectedness of societies in history and the indivisibility of human experience. From this perspective, the ascendancy of the West was not predetermined by its alleged moral and technological superiority, but drew upon the cumulative interaction of humans across Afro-Eurasia throughout history. Hodgson's humanistic conscience and commitment to a nonracialist, nonteleological world history based upon the brotherhood of all humans provide a powerful argument against epistemological nihilists and moral agnostics.

Islam and World History: The Ventures of Marshall Hodgson brings together essays by American, European, and international scholars concerned with both the intellectual legacy and the enduring relevance of Hodgson's vision. The time is ripe for a Hodgson revival. The world of Islam is vast (1.6 billion persons) and complex beyond the imaginings of most Americans; Hodgson's world-historical vision and moral engagement have never been more relevant. As the first volume of critical essays on this important world historian and historian of Islam, this collection aims to bring Hodgson's legacy into the twenty-first century.

Hodgson differed from most other academics of the 1950s and 1960s in that his writings were informed by his radical Quaker consciousness. A conscientious objector to World War II who was interned by the US government, Hodgson was profoundly challenged by the war and its aftermath. The political and moral desolation of the post–World War II era energized him as it did few others. A kerygmatic preacher, he sought to forge a humanistic pedagogy that would change how students/readers thought about cultural others in relation to themselves. The expression of that pedagogy was *The Venture of Islam.*

The revolutionary cosmopolitanism of Hodgson's ideas has brought him the attention of a growing number of readers over the last several decades. This is because of his exacting intellect, as well as his insistence that we locate the history of Islam in the context of other world civilizations. In a present moment dominated by political and moral obtuseness, the breadth of Hodgson's historical vision and his commitment to moral clarity speak across the years to the post-9/11 reader and scholar, whatever her or his specialization.

* * * *

When he died in 1968, Hodgson was on the verge of a major career as the author of an important monograph, a promising start on a third book, and more than a dozen articles.[2] Instead, he is primarily known for his three-volume history of Islamic civilization, *The Venture of Islam: Conscience and History in a World Civilization*, an undergraduate textbook. (As a thought experiment, think of another major scholar whose name is principally associated with a textbook.)

Why does Hodgson continue to have an important claim on our attention? For convenience's sake, it makes sense to think of Hodgson's thought as having four major aspects. These were Hodgson the orientalist, Hodgson the creator of Islamic studies, Hodgson the world historian, and Hodgson the preacher and pedagogue (the kerygmatic Hodgson). Let's briefly consider each of the four avatars of Hodgson, before turning to the essays collected in this book. In this way, we can begin to understand some of the reasons why his work remains current even at fifty years' distance.

HODGSON THE ORIENTALIST

Hodgson was trained in oriental studies at the University of Chicago in the late 1940s. The field tended not to attract moral/ethical epigones. Rather, oriental studies produced philologically trained scholars for whom the text and the oriental language (Greek, Hebrew, Aramaic, Arabic, etc.) were the focuses. Not only did Hodgson have acknowledged language expertise, he also had an unparalleled ability to situate ideas and events in their broader regional and global contexts.

Hodgson's first book, *The Order of Assassins: The Struggle of the Early Nizârî Ismâʿîlîs against the Islamic World*, displayed an impressive understanding of the complex currents of eleventh-century Abbasid history. Deeply immersed in the mystical politics of the Nizari Ismailis, it is a tour de force well-grounded in the complex political and intellectual worlds of thirteenth-century Shiʿism. Had Hodgson's career not been cut short by his untimely death, there is little doubt that a second monograph, signaled by his article "How Did the Early Shîʿa Become Sectarian?" would have cemented his reputation as an orientalist scholar. (For more on this see below.)

HODGSON AND NEW ISLAMIC HISTORY

Instead of another scholarly monograph, however, Hodgson embarked upon the writing of a textbook. When *The Venture of Islam* appeared in 1974, it posed a major challenge to the emergent Islamic field. Unlike his fellow orientalists who were primarily focused upon Islamic authors and their texts, Hodgson thought constantly about the larger cultural and political contexts in which they operated.

However, it is only in *The Venture of Islam* that one sees for the first time the full scope of his ambitious new framework. A first component was his revolutionary new periodization of Islamic history. Instead of the traditional chronology, which had been based upon the concept of an Arab classic age that concluded with overthrow of the Abbasids (1258 CE), Hodgson's new periodization consisted of three main parts, each of which was accorded a volume. Like the previous periodization, the first segment covered the period from the formation of Islam to the classical age of the caliphate (608 to 945 CE). The second volume broke sharply with the earlier approaches, which had viewed the Abbasid era as a classical era and the centuries that followed as the abode of tradition. Conversely, for Hodgson the Middle Periods (945 to 1500) were a high point during which Islam expanded across Eurasia from Morocco to China, becoming a truly universal religion. The third volume took the history from the gunpowder states of the sixteenth and seventeenth centuries (the Ottoman, Safavid, and Mughal Empires) to the present.

Hodgson's new periodization also accomplished a second feat. Rather than viewing Islamic civilization as an essentially Arabian phenomenon, it consistently sought to locate it in the broader context of the history of the other major civilizations of Eurasia, if not of humanity as a whole. Whereas previously historians had difficulty in discussing political and religious change together, Hodgson's dramatic rethinking of Islamic history made it possible to discuss religious and cultural change across cultural boundaries. Still more, it authorized historians to view the internal structure of Islamic history (hitherto linked to the rise and fall of Islamic dynasties) in terms of its social, cultural, and economic dynamics and its hemispheric historical extent. *The Venture of Islam* represents a major enrichment of our understanding, one that has played an important role in the emergence of the new Islamic studies.

HODGSON AND NEW WORLD HISTORY

Hodgson's philosophically engaged and inspiring *Venture of Islam* was informed not only by his reworking of the central themes of classical Islamic history but also by his systematic effort to locate it in world history.

In the 1950s when his project was conceived, the civilizations model of world history in which the contribution of each civilization is discussed independently was still the dominant paradigm. Hodgson's world history began with the notion of the interconnectedness of societies in history and the indivisibility of human experience.[3] From this perspective, the ascendancy of the West was not predetermined by its alleged moral and technological superiority, but drew upon the cumulative interaction of humans.

HODGSON, THE MORALIST AND RADICAL PREACHER

Hodgson, the man of conscience makes academics uneasy. As well he should. Yet his moral commitment, the very thing that for so long made him a semi-pariah in academe, shines a beacon of hope to a new generation of readers interested in alternatives to the present state of the post-9/11 Middle East field. A lifelong Quaker who had publically asserted his pacifist beliefs and borne the consequences, Hodgson was a strong believer in the duty of the moral individual to assert truth to power. "Conscience" for Hodgson was connected to his Quaker faith, and to his belief in the duty of the moral individual to "speak truth to power."

Hodgson's example poses a challenge to the sort of professional scholarship that pretends that it is someone else's job to see the morality of history, or indeed imagines that there can be no morality in an immoral world (and therefore the best thing to do is adopt an urbane nihilism).

At the time when Hodgson's ambitious multivolume textbook was published, to attribute conscience and historical consciousness to Muslims was to challenge centuries of Western prejudice about Islam and Muslims. It also flew in the face of the then common expectations of the direction of modern history, because it was deeply skeptical of the prevailing progressive narrative.

Hodgson's philosophically grounded history derived from postwar thinkers such as Martin Buber, Reinhold Niebuhr, Karl Jaspers, and Paul Tillich (among others). They sought to make religion relevant to the postwar era, and to address the problem of evil in the world and the possibility of hope. At the core of Hodgson's vision was his insistence that Islam be viewed as one of the great civilizational impulses that have marked the course of human history (including Hinduism, Buddhism, Confucianism/Taoism, Judaism, and Christianity).

The Ventures of Marshall Hodgson

In the early 1960s the history of Islam was deeply bound to the dominant Eurocentric narrative, which saw modernity as quintessentially Western and the history of other civilizations (including Islam) as faded glories. As well, professional historians tended to view world history as a deeply problematic enterprise, best exemplified by the woolly-minded metaphysical concerns of Arnold Toynbee and Oswald Spengler. Hodgson's vision led him to drastically recast much of the then-existing chronological framework by inserting Islam into a global context.

The difference, as Moroccan historian Abdesselam Cheddadi insists in his contribution to this volume, could not be greater. Compare for example the title of the first chapter of *Venture* ("The World before Islam") to that of many of the competing textbooks ("Arabia before Muhammad"). Right away the reader is projected into a global narrative, a history in which Islamic civilization is but one civilization among many.

Cheddadi argues that Hodgson's contribution depended upon devising a new conceptual framework for both Islamic history and world history. To understand how revolutionary Hodgson's contributions to both fields were in their own time, Cheddadi suggests, we need to understand that neither would have been possible without the other. He begins by reminding us of the state of both fields at the end of World War II.

The task that Hodgson confronted, Cheddadi avows, was enormous. He had to disengage Islamic history from its orientalist tradition and narrow philological biases while simultaneously devising a conceptually more appropriate framework for world history in which Europe would be viewed as but one of a number of major world civilizations. Only by performing both operations simultaneously would it be possible to relocate the history of modernity within the entire history of humankind and thereby to reevaluate the role of Islamic civilization.

Hodgson's Quaker belief in the unity of humankind and his dissatisfaction with the state of the intellectual field led him to a basic insight: that modernity was a global process that affected all parts of the world at the same time, but to different degrees. The implications of this insight were considerable. Without the cumulative history of the entire Afro-Eurasian Oikoumene (hereafter I use its more familiar English form, *ecumene*) the transformation of the West would have been impossible. Modernity, Hodgson notes, could have happened elsewhere than in the West. And that it first occurred in the West was freighted with enormous consequences. Recognizing this "double enterprise," as Cheddadi calls it, is Hodgson's great achievement. In many respects we have still not caught up with him.

HODGSON'S GHOSTS

Marshall Hodgson's *Venture* has long seemed a splendid anomaly in the context of the American Middle East studies field. As argued above, its call for a world-historical framework attentive to Islam's moral vision was out of step with the then dominant narratives when it was published. Christopher A. Bayly disagrees. In his magisterial contribution, he argues that Hodgson was not as out of step with his time as we might think. Nor was his quest for a moralistic history as far from us.

Bayly begins by noting that the global crisis that culminated in 1914 with the outbreak of World War I was preceded by a growing European sense that spirituality had been crushed by the materialism of the modern age and was no longer to be sought in Europe. Instead, many Europeans looked to the spiritual heritage of the East. Bayly surveys the work of intellectuals, both European and Asian, who pursued this line of thinking in the first half of the twentieth century. He aptly compares Hodgson's approach to that of French orientalist Louis Massignon (1883–1962), whose mysticism and generous moral vision of Islamic civilization most resembles his own.

Why has Hodgson had so slight an impact upon British intellectuals in the post-1950 era, Bayly asks. One reason, he suggests, was the residual power of Marxism in the 1950s–1970s, which rendered Hodgson's emphasis on civilizations illegible, even though his global vision and residual materialism might in retrospect have appealed. British orientalists of the period also appear not to know him, their greatest collective achievement being the *echt* orientalist *Cambridge History of Islam*.

Given Hodgson's obscurity in his own lifetime, the great puzzle for Bayly is why many Asian and world historians urge their students to read him. Is it perhaps because "they mourn the purging of moral judgment and idealism from their subject"? He leaves the question hanging. In some respects, he opines, Hodgson anticipates Samuel P. Huntington's rediscovery of civilizations as the essential cultural context in which change happens. "Despite the internal conflicts within Hodgson's thought," Bayly concludes, "current events have tended to confirm his view that historical change, for most of human history, has to be understood as a pattern of adaptation across the whole Afro-Eurasian Ecumene." Other contributors to this volume would agree.

* * * *

The English historian Edward Gibbon's *History of the Decline and Fall of the Roman Empire* may seem an unlikely comparison to Hodgson's *Venture*. Yet, as Robert Mankin argues, the two have much in common. Little known to non–Gibbon aficionados, *Decline and Fall* was not just about the Roman Empire. Rather, Mankin notes, in its final form Gibbon's history covered the period

96–1788 CE, making it a kind of world history both in its coverage and in Gibbon's growing insistence that historical sequences and facts (and not just general history) mattered.

But how did Gibbon become a world historian? In his essay on Gibbon and Hodgson, Mankin suggests that Gibbon's view of world history derived from the French Enlightenment idea of "*histoire générale*," according to which geography and space were central. Mankin's interest in Hodgson was originally sparked by the latter's essay "The Interrelations of Societies in History," for its denunciation of the Eurocentrism inherent in the Mercator projection map.[4]

The contexts in which Gibbon and Hodgson wrote, he states, shaped the kinds of history they both wrote. Writing during the period of the French Revolution, Gibbon saw many of his formative understandings challenged by the dramatic political changes of the period. Hodgson wrote in the aftermath of the World War II period, which was marked by the onset of the Cold War and the collapse of European colonial empires. Despite these differences, both individuals saw themselves as "philosophic historians," an important axis of similarity. Here Mankin brings his training as a specialist on the eighteenth century to his understanding of Hodgson's philosophical framework, noting, for example, coded references to Montesquieu and Hume.

There's more to the Gibbon/Hodgson comparison. As a young student at Oxford, Gibbon converted to Catholicism, which got him kicked out of school (then reserved for Anglicans). Sent away to boarding school in Switzerland, he began the study of Arabic, but was told by his tutor that becoming an orientalist was not for the likes of him. Mankin sees in this the beginning of Gibbon's determination to tell the story of the decline of Rome in the broadest possible way, including in the scope of his concerns Byzantium and the land of Islam. In his comparison of Gibbon and Hodgson the reader is led to consider their joint quest for intercultural dialogue. It is a most stimulating peregrination.

HODGSON AND THE NEW WORLD HISTORY

The principal impediment to the development of a world history worthy of the name was the tendency for humans to think about the human past in function of the past of their people, their civilization. These centrisms (as we can call them) on the one hand induce the tendency to see the self as axiomatic, and the other (any other) as necessarily derivative of the self. (Throw in the idea of progress, and you've got modernization theory!) On the other hand, the idea of civilization seems to summon up essentialisms, both of the self and the other. *We* are (pick your favorite key traits), while *they* are (pick some less desirable traits). Throw in universal history as a philosophically reified conception, and you will find yourself in some ahistorical space deprived of the ability to think about the relations of societies in history. To understand this is to begin to appreciate the magnitude of Hodgson's contribution to world history. It is the subject of several of the contributions to this book.

But how did Hodgson make his breakthrough? Michael Geyer urges us to consider the ethical and political context in which Hodgson forged his ideas. In his challenging essay Geyer introduces us to the young Hodgson and explains how a midwestern Quaker young man in the early 1940s grew into a militant pacifist and radical nonviolent internationalist. The solution to the problems made manifest in World War II, Hodgson came to believe, was an epistemic break: that the people of the world understand that they were members of a real, existing world community. With that change in consciousness came the need to change the world accordingly. For Hodgson, world history was not a career, but a political calling.

Geyer traces the evolution of Hodgson's conception of world history and his continual dissatisfaction with it (since it was apprehended on the intellectual plane only, and not made the basis for self-transformation). Hodgson stressed three points: the necessity to deprovincialize the United States, to decenter Europe, and to de-orientalize Asia ("There is no Orient," he proclaimed, anticipating Edward Said by more than thirty years). World history was equal parts unlearning provincialism and learning the story of world development from the world point of view (that is, by the critical comparative method).

Most surprisingly, Geyer's essay leads us to the conclusion that it was Hodgson's religious radicalism which propelled him into conceiving of Afro-Eurasian history as a connected commons, an interactive entity that can be studied empirically. But instead of this debouching on a transhistory of migration and exchange (the current norm in the world history field), Hodgson was fired with the creative energy inherent in "life-orientational systems." Geyer urges us to understand that at the heart of Hodgson's approach was "a dialectic of internal and external settlement and unsettlement." What the young conscientious objector Hodgson had been about, he reminds us, was changing the world. The aim of his youthful "Handbook of World Citizenship" was to combat provincialism (and not to change the other in our own image). Based upon the Marshall G. S. Hodgson Papers at the Regenstein Library at the University of Chicago, Geyer's essay plunges us deeply into Hodgson's diagnosis of what needed to be changed and how world history, properly understood, could bring it about. Geyer's essay is a crucial send-off for readers seeking a Hodgson booster shot.

* * * *

Until now Marshall Hodgson has primarily been seen as a product of the intellectual environment at the University of Chicago during the 1940s and 1950s. In her contribution, "Decentering World History: Marshall Hodgson and the UNESCO Project," Katja Naumann agrees that there was something special about the University of Chicago context. However, on the basis of her deep reading of the relevant personal papers and institutional archives of the university's principals, Naumann urges us to expand our field of vision.

She suggests that almost as important was Hodgson's little-known editorial role in the six-volume UNESCO-sponsored Scientific and Cultural History of Mankind (SCHM). The editor of volume 4, *The Foundations of the Modern World, 1300–1775*, Louis Gottschalk, was a member of Hodgson's department and appointed him to help edit this deeply problematic volume. This experience, Naumann suggests, was intellectually crucial to Hodgson's break with the nation-centered and Eurocentric approaches to world history. It is in editing the SCHM, she argues, that Hodgson developed the world-historical framework that he was later to deploy to great effect in *Venture*. She documents his encounters with international scholars such as the South Asian historians Jawaharlal Nehru and Ramesh Chandra Majumdar, Mexican historian Silvio Zavala, Chinese historian B. Kwok, and Soviet historian Evgenij M. Zhukov.

In addition to Hodgson's participation in the UNESCO project, Naumann notes his attendance at several international historical conventions, notably Stockholm (1960) and Vienna (1965). There he encountered leading Soviet and Asian historians. From the discussions and debates at these conferences Hodgson forged the conviction that "the decentering of world history and the integration of non-European history" was an imperative for the field.

* * * *

In contrast with other Western historians of Islam in the postwar era, Marshall Hodgson was not only a well-trained orientalist but also a bold conceptual thinker. As Pamela Crossley's essay suggests, his work was in many respects ahead of his time. Crossley is a leading historian of Central Asia and China. In process of studying the larger history of Asian steppe empires in the fourteenth to seventeenth centuries, she was led to Hodgson's discussion of

Islamic steppe empires in *Venture,* in which his concept of the "military patronage state" figures large. Hodgson was struck by the use of patronage (that is, the transfer of important real and symbolic tokens of wealth and power) by Mongol rulers to maintain their legitimacy in the eyes of urban and religious elites of conquered populations.

Following Hodgson, Crossley views the imperial household and its patronage relationships with military elites as generative of specific forms of centralization across Eurasia. She argues that viewing the Ming and Qing dynasties as military patronage states reveals the presence of numerous practices associated with the Mongol patronage state. Her argument ultimately is more complex. For she suggests that while the Mongol legacy was one formative element of these empires, it was not the only one. They also drew in important ways upon the heritage of the Chinese imperial system, including the emperor, and the Confucian legal and ethical traditions.

In her conclusion Crossley carefully considers the range and applicability of the term both to Islamic states and to Mongol-style regimes. In this way she is led to identify the presence of elements of the Mongol patronage system in the Russia of the Romanovs and the India of the Mughals. Thus Hodgson's concept proves relevant across Eurasia in the fourteenth through seventeenth centuries. "Eurasian historical studies," Crossley concludes, "is substantially deepened with the restoration of military patronage as a foundation discourse in early modern state centralization."

HODGSON AND THE NEW ISLAMIC HISTORY

Since Marshall Hodgson is best known as a historian of the Islamic world, it may be a surprise to learn that some see him as a prescient analyst of gender and sexuality in Islam. So argues Jocelyne Dakhlia in her important contribution to this book, "Harems and Cathedrals: The Question of Gender and Sexuality in the Work of Marshall Hodgson." While gender and sexuality constitute one of the most important but least-known aspects of his intellectual legacy, she argues, it is high time they receive the attention they deserve.

Dakhlia begins her essay with a lengthy discussion of Hodgson's distinction (*Venture,* vol. 2) between what he calls the contractual basis of Islamdom and the hierarchical basis of occidental society; in "Cultural Models in Islamdom and the Occident," Hodgson contrasts what he calls the egalitarian and contractual character of the Muslim household (as guaranteed by the sharia) and the hierarchical organizational principle of occidental society. Here Hodgson systematically explores questions relative to the family, kinship, and sexuality as they play out across the Irano-Mediterranean lands. His approach is a kind of a comparative structurally oriented historical anthropology that while sometimes abstract and complex, is never less than brilliant.

Dakhlia next turns to Hodgson's discussion of the place of slavery (especially female slaves) in Muslim society and Western society—not necessarily to the advantage of the latter. In his view the status of the individual, male or female, was personal, and not a function of his or her place in a legally restricted social hierarchy. Dakhlia concludes the section with the question: is Hodgson an Islamic feminist? This prompts a brilliant consideration of his relationship to the literature of his time, but also to the work of Islamic feminists such as Fatima Mernissi.

Dakhlia opines that Hodgson's systematic evaluation of all aspects of Islamic belief and practice pushed him to develop his thought far beyond that of his contemporaries. It is Hodgson's egalitarian reading of Islam that led him to raise the question of the relations of gender, the sexes, and homosexuality in Islamic societies in ways that still resonate with current scholarship. Since there is little evidence that Hodgson's personal beliefs differed greatly from the heteronormative American male of the period, his views of male homosexuality in Muslim societies come as a surprise. In a thoughtful comparison of Hodgson's views of Muslim homosexuality with that of the contemporary scholarly literature, Dakhlia remarks on his "astonishing analytical lucidity and a surprisingly up-to-date scientific understanding." Once more Hodgson was there first.

In a lengthy concluding section, Dakhlia provides a carefully nuanced exegesis of Hodgson's discussion of Islamic decline in *Venture*. She shows that as a world historian, he would strongly resist the essentialism of works such as Bernard Lewis's *What Went Wrong?* (2002). Although Hodgson tended to resist the developmentalism that was hegemonic in his time, he reflects the debates among contemporary Muslim intellectuals about the education of women and the structural instability deriving from polygamy. However, Dakhlia insists, Hodgson's forceful anthropological and historical decompartmentalization resists any easy resolution. "Hodgson's approach," she urges, "in many ways confirm[s] the centrality of the issue of gender as far as it is historicized and historically construed—thereby escaping an ahistorical, old-fashioned, and generally agreed-upon anthropology (so common when it comes to Islam)." Her demonstration is a tour de force.

* * * *

In his contribution, "The Problem of Muslim Universality," Faisal Devji performs a similarly complex and nuanced critique of Hodgson's use of the concepts of race and civilization in *Venture*. Devji begins by noting that while allegedly universal, both concepts lacked institutional support other than the fact of European empire. This made them the object of critique by indigenous intellectuals, among them Gandhi, who pointed out their self-justifying parochialism as a way of critiquing European claims for equality and universalism.

This is where Devji sees the relevance of Hodgson. Far from Hodgson's being a defender of Islamic civilization (making him a "civilizationist" in today's coded academic language), a close reading of *Venture* shows that he held a rather different view. Hodgson believed that by 1945 all civilizations were similarly detached from their agrarian origins and thus equally exposed to modern cultural trends. He also believed that among world civilizations Islam was the only one besides the West that was truly universal. Its fate in the modern era was crucial for humanity as a whole. This observation prompts Devji to remark: "More than a history of Islamic civilization, then, or even a comparative or world history, Hodgson's intellectual project in *Venture* might be seen as providing us with a non-Western genealogy of modernity and our global present."

Devji concludes with a close examination of his affinity for the thought of Hodgson and Muhammad Iqbal (d. 1938), whom some still consider the most important thinker of modern Islam. Devji carefully unpacks the similarities and differences of each man's thoughts about Islam and modernity and its place in global history. A key dimension of his discussion turns on the place of Islam's esoteric tradition, which was the chief mode by which premodern Muslims could claim universality, rather than its sacred law. For Devji the comparison with Iqbal allows us to better understand Hodgson's view of the place of Islam in modern times.

* * * *

When Hodgson embarked upon his career (he died in 1968), both world history and Islamic history were still deeply embedded in an essentially Eurocentric and present-centered intellectual world. This mental framework made it difficult for contemporaries to grasp the stakes in World War II, the horrors that attended it, or the necessity of the movement of decolonization that followed it. The essays in this book constitute a kind of necessary stocktaking that allows us to grasp Hodgson's brilliance and originality, as well as the extent to which he was still shaped by the ideas and presuppositions that affected his generation.

In the Cold War atmosphere of the 1950s, to dispute that "the West" was the center of the modern world and the source of progress smacked of anti-Americanism. Having lived in South Asia and traveled in the Middle East, Hodgson had come to distrust claims of Western superiority. His skepticism about modernity, which differed both from Cold War Western modernizationism and from Soviet state-led development, remains prescient. The underlying assumptions about Islam, the West, and the course of modern history challenged by Hodgson in his magnum opus have remained constant.

Read together, the essays in this book make clear three things; the complexity of the mental world of Hodgson's generation (and the daring of his ideas), the reasons why his writings both on Islam and on world history (after initially eliciting great praise) were pushed to one side, and finally, the extent to which his ideas and especially his morally engaged stance are of relevance to us once again today.

Notes

1. Marshall G. S. Hodgson, *The Venture of Islam: Conscience and History in a World Civilization*, 3 vols. (Chicago: University of Chicago Press, 1974).

2. Marshall G. S. Hodgson, *The Order of Assassins: The Struggle of the Early Nizârî Ismâ'îlîs against the Islamic World* ('s Gravenhage: Mouton, 1955).

3. See the essays collected in Marshall G. S. Hodgson, *Rethinking World History: Essays on Europe, Islam, and World History*, ed. Edmund Burke III (Cambridge: Cambridge University Press, 1993).

4. Included in Hodgson, *Rethinking*, 3–28.

CHAPTER TWO

Islamic History and World History

THE DOUBLE ENTERPRISE OF MARSHALL G. S. HODGSON

Abdesselam Cheddadi

TRANSLATED BY EDMUND BURKE III

Around the middle of the twentieth century, historians' conceptions of the history of Islam and its place in world history began to undergo a considerable transformation. Chronologically it had by then become clearer that Islamic history constituted the link between ancient history and modern history. Spatially it had also become clearer that Islamic civilization, which had developed in the heart of Afro-Eurasia, was the first historical bridge linking the two extremities of the zone of premodern agrarian civilization that extended from Gibraltar to China. Marshall G. S. Hodgson was the uncontested initiator and most brilliant actor in bringing about this transformation.

When he died in 1968 at the age of forty-seven he left two major works unpublished that had simultaneously occupied him for more than twenty years: one on Islamic history, the other on world history. Thanks to the dedication of his colleague Reuben Smith, the first manuscript, which was the furthest along, was published posthumously under the title *The Venture of Islam* in 1974.[1] It was immediately celebrated as a work of major importance: rich, complex, and reflective of a crucial moral engagement. The second work was less fortunate. "The Unity of World History" has still not found a publisher and, as one of his admirers affirmed, is unlikely to do so "despite the enormous potential that it represents."[2] In any event, the two works, written at the same time, represent two indissoluble aspects of Hodgson's research and reflection. For methodological as well as factual reasons he found it impossible to discuss one without the other.

To begin with, it is important to understand that it was not until the 1960s that world history as a discipline had begun to emerge from the disdain and indifference in which it had been held by most professional historians. Its enormous prestige during the European Enlightenment did not survive the Age of Revolutions and the growing importance of the nation-state that followed. By the end of the nineteenth century, historians were primarily interested in national histories, often with a chauvinistic and European exceptionalist emphasis. Even the momentum that had been given to world history by Oswald Spengler and Arnold Toynbee after World War I was unable to break down the resistance of specialists, who continued to see it as a pastime for dilettantes. But beginning in the 1960s other factors combined to give it renewed appeal. The end of empire and with it, the retreat of Western Eurocentrism, along with the rise to a renewed sense of global interdependence, fostered the appearance of work on transcultural interactions and led to a rich harvest of comparative studies.

Hodgson and his colleague at the University of Chicago, William H. McNeill, were closely associated with this renewal. The latter's major work, *The Rise of the West,* appeared in 1964, around the time Hodgson was completing *The Venture of Islam.*[3] The two historians had several common objectives: to separate world history from the ideological and metaphysical grounding of their prestigious predecessors Spengler and Toynbee; to rethink modernity by locating it in the context of all of human history and finally by basing their approach upon the new anthropological knowledge. This said, one must recognize that their points of departure, especially about the place of Europe in world history, were divergent. McNeill, as his title suggests, was less successful in extricating the subject from its prior Eurocentric swaddling clothes. By contrast, by locating himself in a perspective outside of Europe, Hodgson gave himself the means to develop a more truly global view of world history. His impact on Islamic history was equally revolutionary. By taking it out of the narrow straightjacket into which the orientalist tradition had placed it, he was able to shake off the dust of ages, to enrich it and to direct it down previously untrodden paths. Alas, fifty years after his death, these remain largely unexplored.

Hodgson's vision broke with the traditional approaches to the study of Islam in three major ways: conceptual, geographical, and chronological. The conceptual break was marked by the critique of orientalism forms of knowledge, and more generally of European presuppositions about world history. As a confirmed professional orientalist Hodgson undertook a radical critique of his own discipline. Those writing in the scholarly tradition of the nineteenth and early twentieth century believed that civilizations derived from unchanging essences, often tied to their languages, which could be in turn derived from their major texts.[4] Expanding the field of investigation to the most varied materials, including making a major place for archaeology, Hodgson sought to question not just the texts but the contexts in which they existed in order to uncover the interplay of other cultures. Hodgson preached a method grounded in empathy and the respect of the subject in an effort to understand it from the inside, to more fully enter into its own perspective. Here he can be seen as following in the footsteps of the French orientalist Louis Massignon, although he eschewed the latter's mysticism. On this, both scholars were under the influence of Carl Jung and Wilhelm Dilthey, upon whose principle of *verstehen* they based their works.[5]

A second determining aspect of Hodgson's approach was of an ethical order. Filled with pacifist and philanthropic convictions due to his Quaker faith, Hodgson had an abiding faith in the fraternity and equality of all people. The human species as a whole appeared to him as the only field of discourse for any humanly defensible research. The epigraph of John Woolman, a Quaker pacificist and antislavery advocate of the eighteenth century, with which he begins *The Venture of Islam* is highly significant of his anti-Eurocentric attitude: "To consider mankind other than brethren, to think that favours are peculiar to one nation and exclude others, plainly supposes a darkness in the understanding." These premises allow him to engage the history of Islam differently. Forging his own terminology, putting to work his own critical historical and geographic concepts, he sought to study Islamic civilization as a part of universal human heritage and to demonstrate its importance in the context of a world history recentered upon Asia, the birthplace of agrarianate-citied life. In order to orient his analyses, he proposed reliance upon an ensemble of ideal types associated with the major phases of this civilization (on which he espoused a methodology similar to that identified with the sociologist/historian Max Weber).

The second break with previous studies of Islam that marks Hodgson's approach was geographic. It resulted in an expansion of the field of Islamic history to incorporate the entire space touched by Islam, while displacing the center of gravity from the Arab Middle East to Irano-Turkish Asia. One of the chief obstacles that had prevented earlier scholars from understanding Islamic history in its entirety, he observes, was what he called is "Arabistic bias." Both European and Arab scholars had the tendency to focus upon the original centers of Islam and to stop with the Arab phase of Islamic history. Another tendency with unfortunate consequences for Islamic studies lay in admitting Islam into world history only when it was in collision with Europe.

Finally, Hodgson's third major point of rupture with prior knowledge concerns his chronology and periodization of Islamic history. A consequence of the two prior points of cleavage, it is perhaps the most important. Hodgson's division of Islamic history into three parts (formative period, middle period, and the period of gunpowder empires and modern times) allowed him to highlight the fundamental importance both for the history of Islam and for world history of the period extending from the decline of the Abbasid empire as a bureaucratic empire (c. 945 CE) until the appearance of the great Turkish, Persian, and Mughal empires of the sixteenth century, which in the orientalist tradition had previously been considered as a period of decadence.[6] In fact it was in the "Middle Periods" (as he called them) that Islam made a crucial leap forward on a hemispheric scale, creating the greatest cosmopolitan society in history, a multilingual society (with the emergence alongside of Arabic of Turkish, Persian, and, later, Urdu as languages of culture), based upon the separation of state and society and the growing importance of a lettered class, as well as on the spread of Sufism. In the process it brought down the walls separating regional civilizations in Afro-Eurasia and gave birth to some of the most celebrated historical figures in culture, science, and art in Islamic civilization (notably Ibn Sina, Ibn al-ʿArabi, al-Ghazali, al-Biruni, and al-Ferdowsi).

Hodgson thus accomplished two amazing feats—writing a history of Islam disconnected from the dominant Eurocentrist narrative and adopting a world-historical viewpoint. Breaking with the older tradition of privileging the great military generals, statesmen, and empire builders, he introduces the reader to the mental universe of Islamic civilization. This enabled him to give the reader a close-up view of the major cultural, spiritual, social, and political figures of Islamic history, now seen with a certain closeness and familiarity. By attempting to include Islamic civilization in its entirety, he managed in addition to bring to our attention the world system constructed by Islam circa 1200 CE, a system which in a certain manner prefigures our own while being constructed on radically different principles. While the modern world system is essentially focused on *Homo economicus*, the Islamic system in contrast was constructed around a book, the Quran, and its double requirement of establishing a just social order and bringing men closer to their Creator. It found its coherence and solidarity from the common values that it incarnated and maintained from the informal links between merchants, scholars, and saints.

The study of Islamic history freed it from the essentialist conceptions that put forward binary oppositions such as East/West, Tradition/Modernity, and recentered it on the premodern agrarianate-citied system of premodern Eurasia.

This allowed Hodgson to make important advances in his conception of world history and to propose a whole series of key postulates: that the history of civilization was Asia-centric and that it was based upon interdependent interregional developments on a hemispheric scale, especially phenomena that crossed regional frontiers, such as the diffusion of Indian forms of monasticism. One of his fundamental axioms was that discoveries in any part of the world eventually diffused throughout the other agrarianate-literate civilizations, thereby transforming the possibilities of human action throughout the world.

In closing, it is worth insisting upon two points at the center of Hodgson's preoccupations: the place of Europe in world history and the nature of modernity. For Hodgson Islamic civilization was a sister civilization of European civilization and shared with it the same Irano-Semitic roots and the same base in Hellenistic thought, west Asian prophetic monotheism, and the political system of agrarian bureaucratic empires. In this way *The Venture of Islam* necessarily provokes a reexamination of European history, which, relocated in the context of world history, cannot but lose its exceptional character.

A second major conclusion of Hodgson's approach to world history is also clear: viewed through a world-historical lens, Europe no longer appears as the inevitable consequence of the working out of its own internal rhythms: "Without the cumulative history of the entire Afro-Eurasian Ecumene the transformation of the West would have been almost impossible."[7] The assertion of a line that connects the ancient Greeks to the Renaissance to modern times is therefore nothing more than an optical illusion, nourished by an overly selective historical imagination. Rather, it was axiomatic for Hodgson that modernity was a global process that affected all parts of the world at the same time, though in different degrees. From this it follows that the globalization about which so much ink is spilled these days is not a recent phenomenon. The prehistory of all of humanity constitutes on the contrary an underlying essential condition of our modernity. If Europe initiated the process of modernization, this was far from predestined. Given the relative equality of agrarianate-literate societies and the tendency for cultural innovations to diffuse around the ecumene over a period more or less long, modernity could have arisen elsewhere, in China or the Islamic world. Wherever it arose, modernity would have been a global event.

To conclude: whatever we do, whatever we say, we are all modern: the rupture with our premodern pasts, wherever we are, is definitive. We must accept this rupture in conceiving of our links to the human past not as an impossible continuity, but as a game of construction and deconstruction eternally restarted. Likewise we must accept that each people, each human group, each person brings his own contribution, and that our pasts are parts of a shared and global past. Hodgson's examination of the particular case of Islamic history can only be understood in the context of that of the entire world, as part of the double enterprise of Islamic history and world history.

Notes

1. Marshall G. S. Hodgson, *The Venture of Islam: Conscience and History in a World Civilization*, 3 vols. (Chicago: University of Chicago Press, 1974).

2. It must be mentioned that a number of sections of *Venture* together with chapters from this unpublished work have been included in Marshall G. S. Hodgson, *Rethinking World History: Essays on Europe, Islam, and World History*, ed. Edmund Burke III (Cambridge: Cambridge University Press, 1993). See Burke's introduction, p. xii.

3. William H. McNeill, *The Rise of the West: A History of the Human Community* (Chicago: University of Chicago Press, 1964).

4. On this point, see the illuminating remarks of Maurice Olender on the particular example of the "Aryans" and the "Semites" in *Les langues du paradis: Aryens et Sémites, un couple providentiel* (Paris: Éditions du Seuil, 1994).

5. Hodgson, *Rethinking*, 304.

6. Hodgson proposes another, more detailed periodization. See *L'Islam dans l'histoire mondiale*, trans. Abdesselam Cheddadi (Paris: Sindbad/Actes Sud, 1998), chap. 4, p. 189, n. 14.

7. Hodgson, *Venture*, 3:198.

Hodgson's Ghosts

CHAPTER THREE

From Gibbon to Hodgson and Back

Robert J. Mankin

> Perhaps the Arabs might not find in a single historian, so clear and comprehensive a narrative of their own exploits, as that which will be deduced in the ensuing sheets.
>
> —Edward Gibbon, *The History of the Decline and Fall of the Roman Empire*, 1788[1]

In the course of studying Gibbon's great work, *The History of the Decline and Fall of the Roman Empire*, one almost always takes to wondering why Gibbon stretched the horizons of his account so far in time and space. The *Decline* was published in six volumes between 1776 and 1788, but what matters just as much is that it covers a period from, roughly, 96 to 1452 CE or slightly after, and that its geographic reach extends from Rome and Constantinople to Britain, Scandinavia, Russia, and North Africa, and through the Middle East to Central Asia, if not quite fully to India and China. The *Decline* did not aspire to be Braudelian *histoire de la longue durée* or Voltairean *histoire générale*. But Gibbon's project almost naturally inclined him to a version of world history. Some of his earliest reading as a (precocious) child had been in the universal histories of the late seventeenth century, and well beyond the theological underpinnings of such writings, he developed a powerful interest in the Far East, India, the Middle East, and, most of all, Islam. Much later, he read Voltaire's *Essai sur les mœurs* (1769) under one—or several—of its earlier titles, *Essai sur l'histoire universelle* (1754) or *Essai sur l'histoire générale* (1756). He would quip of Voltaire many years later: "His account . . . contains, as usual, much general sense and truth, with some particular errors" (*Decline* 3:796n20). The remark was indulgent though ultimately damning for Voltaire the historian. As his career went on, Gibbon was less and less interested in *general* sense and more and more in *historical* sense, of which accuracy was an essential part.[2]

Gibbon and Hodgson: An Imaginary Conversation

For many readers, the most common way of thinking about Gibbon's inclination for world history is to wonder *why* he wrote about the Eastern Empire of Rome, for which he expressed little apparent sympathy or sense of affinity. Indeed, he calls Byzantine civilization a world of "dead uniformity" and "copious barrenness" (*Decline* 3:24–25). The great classicist Arnaldo Momigliano could imagine only that the passage by way of Byzantium allowed Gibbon to enrich his sense of what "decline and fall" really entailed for a civilization:

> In Bisanzio Gibbon cerca soltanto la decadenza e perciò trova soltanto la decadenza. Ciò che piuttosto è curioso, perche contradittorio, è che questa decadenza è statica. Questo impero che non muore mai, o almeno sopravvive di mille anni al suo gemello occidentale, sembra resistere a tutta le facezie di Gibbon. I bizantinisti di età più recente che vanno in direzione opposta alla ricerca di una spiegazione per la vitalità di Bisanzio, sono i più aspri critici di Gibbon.[3]

One critic, the great Byzantinist Steven Runciman, took Gibbon very literally and labored to defend Byzantium from what he considered unfair and inaccurate accusations,[4] whereas the question might have been why it got so much treatment at all. In any case, my route has been slightly different. In wondering about how and why the *Decline* opened itself to a new understanding of geography and space, it became necessary for me to try to identify Gibbon's idea of Europe and how that fit within the larger field of the Eurasian continent. Some years ago, in the course of that effort, I happened on Hodgson's essays criticizing the Mercator projection and then on *The Venture of Islam*. The latter struck me, to use the kind of phrase Gibbon was coining in the eighteenth century, as a classic performance—though I had to ask myself at once how it could be that *Venture* was so little known as a classic. This is a point I'll come back to at the end of my remarks.

In any case, I began to suspect that Gibbon and Hodgson would have had a great deal to say to each other. It was not just a matter of world history. For instance, another milestone of the same period and the same university, Chicago professor William McNeill's *Rise of the West* (1964), refers to Gibbon several times but clearly there is no special relation at work, no *atome crochu* between their visions or methods. But with Hodgson I gradually picked up signs of how a conversation might have taken shape. One of the oddities of the *Decline* lies in the fact that Gibbon was extraordinarily apprehensive about what the public would make of his first volume, published in 1776 and covering the years 96 to 313 CE. And so in the preface to the *Decline*, as if to dangle a carrot before his readers' eyes, he brashly detailed what his full-scale "plan" would be. If the readers wanted Gibbon to tell the *whole*, coherent story of Rome's decline and fall, they would have to encourage him to write on and on. Gibbon calculated it would be necessary to study not two hundred years but "about thirteen centuries," and these, he felt, could be broken down into three distinct periods. The second, which extended from Justinian to Charlemagne, was the most distinctive of the three. It was more detailed and also provided the most integrated view of East and West:

> II. The second period of the Decline and Fall of Rome may be supposed to commence with the reign of Justinian, who, by his laws, as well as by his victories, restored a transient splendor to the Eastern Empire. It will comprehend the invasion of Italy by the Lombards; the conquest of the Asiatic and African provinces by the Arabs, who embraced the religion of Mahomet; the revolt of the Roman people against the feeble princes of Constantinople; and the elevation of Charlemagne, who, in the year eight hundred, established the second, or German Empire of the West. (*Decline*, 1:1–2, preface)

The first volume of the *Decline* turned out to be an immediate success, leaving Gibbon now free to execute his plan in three parts—which in time became six massive volumes. Arithmetically, that amounted to about two centuries per volume. It is a coincidence worth noting that Hodgson considered just that as the proper scale for historical perception. In *Venture* he observed, "The autonomous internal development of the various traditions that make up a culture comes clearer if we take as our periods one, two, or even perhaps three centuries together."[5] What is more, we have to admire the regularity and precision with which Gibbon carried out his mammoth project, though we also need to recognize that something went very wrong in the part I've just cited. It took Gibbon a whole extra volume to reach the end of his first part, and by the time he did, chronological order had broken down or, to put it more neutrally, given way to other principles of narrative organization. So it was that Charlemagne appeared before Mahomet and, more importantly for today, certain forces detained Gibbon and prevented him from giving full scope to the larger, articulated interregional history he might have been able to write.

What were those forces? I would say they had to do with literary and political culture, specifically, the relevance of writing western Europe's regional history for a western European readership. Politics will come later in the chapter; let me focus for a second on the "literary." For Gibbon's early modern world, "literature" meant "learning" or "skill in letters."[6] So we must expand the literary to mean the character of public discourse and knowledge, to which Gibbon's historical method gave a new, worldly scope as broad as his field of vision allowed. That method, to summarize it briefly, involved the collation and analysis of *all* the available texts, and the meta-expansion of that analysis in a vast number of footnotes that reflected on and refracted the main argument. Gibbon's broadly literary-epistemological innovation perfectly suited the publishing market of his times, for there had been a remarkable growth throughout British society of a demand for historical narrative. (Consequently, a lot of money became available to those writing history.)[7] So Gibbon wrote for a general public that he took to be interested in its own historical, cultural, and religious origins, and educable, as well as to a discursive community of scholars across Europe whose languages—especially Latin, French, and Italian—could also be made useful to the general public in certain circumstances. Accordingly, Gibbon delved deeper and deeper into the details of *intra*regional, Western history. That is another way of saying that he got seriously behind schedule. The three last volumes of the *Decline,* which include the origin and rise of Islam, are in some ways a magnificent and highly controlled race against time. It was important he keep his promise to his reader of the world.

Despite that haste, I take it that Hodgson saw Gibbon as a bona fide interlocutor for Islamic and world history and that he would have understood the earnestness of Gibbon's historic confidence that I cited in opening this essay. *Venture* and what I know of Hodgson's other writings mention Gibbon no more often than does McNeill,[8] but what a great difference there is between the two! The most telling allusion in Hodgson is implicit, when he refers to *himself* via Gibbon's trademark persona, the philosophic historian. The latter was probably a term of Gibbon's invention that he had begun by applying to Tacitus (*Decline* 1:230), though he no doubt felt he had earned the right to it as well. Did Hodgson? Here is a characteristic sentence from his unfinished work, "The Unity of World History": "And surely a philosophic historian may be glad for information which helps him to trace the unfolding of an idea, the essence of a situation, beyond the limits imposed by the consciousness of contemporary actors."[9] In Gibbon's understanding of history, "information" was never exactly at issue. His method often entailed getting to the "essence of a situation" via the slight, even trivial detail, without needing to command a whole body of (often unavailable) information. In this sense, if Hodgson too was a philosophic historian, his philosophy was rooted in the methodology of the social sciences and a strain of positivism that could express itself in the collection of "data,"[10] and in terms such as these: "We know that the question determines the answer: what questions we ask set the range within which we can even look for data, and—in just that degree to which the question is univalent—sets the answer that objective and persistent inquiry will come to" (*Rethinking* 256). We can infer from things Gibbon said in his autobiographical writings that his method would have been to compare the kinds of answers that different people might give to a single question, and thus to *expand* on the valences of the question and to create conditions of dialogue among the answers or results. I am tempted to award Gibbon the methodological high ground here, though in some ways Hodgson would have understood and even perhaps agreed. And when it comes to actual practice, it seems fairly certain that in spite of his normativity, Hodgson gauged better than Gibbon ever could "the peculiarly eccentric character of the West" (*Rethinking* 265).

But allow me to stay manichaean for a minute more: with positivism versus reflexivity we have a first and rather contrasting sense of the two men as philosophic historians. Luckily, the matter can be taken further, in ways that enrich the conversation. As if he too had been overly normative, Gibbon repented at the end of his life for mistaken ideas regarding what *we* would call the genre of world history. We see this in the way he annotated his personal copy of the *Decline*. His first bit of soul-searching singled out the opening paragraph of the entire work, where he had ringingly declaimed the importance of his subject: Rome's "decline and fall," he told potential readers in 1776, was "a revolution which will ever be remembered, and is still felt by the nations of the earth" (*Decline* 1:31).[11] In 1791, certain of having a readership, he regretted having been so pompous in his rhetoric and so Eurocentric in his history. He thought to tone the sentence down by limiting the repercussions of Rome's decline to "our own, and the neighbouring countries of Europe" even as he asked himself in the margins, "Have Asia and Africa, from Japan to Morocco, any feeling or memory of the Roman Empire?" (*Decline* 1:31, 3:1094). The world, he was saying, was vaster and less attuned to the West than his language had allowed. Another annotation sounds "Hodgsonian" in the way that it tries to disentangle the points of the compass: "The distinction of North and South is real and intelligible; and our pursuit is terminated on either side by the poles of the Earth. But the difference of East and West is arbitrary, and shifts round the globe. As the men of the North not of the West the legions of Gaul and Germany were superior to the *south*-eastern natives of Asia and Egypt. It is the triumph of cold over heat; which may however and has been surmounted by moral causes" (3:1095; Gibbon's emphasis).

Surely these late invocations of Montesquieu on climate theory and Hume on moral causes do not end in the synthesis of major thinkers who influenced him, but the point is that Gibbon was again reflecting on the limits of his world and looking for useful terms for comparison and interrelation of its parts. In addition, his rhetorical question about "Asia and Africa" was more resonant than any positive answer could have been. That reminds us that Gibbon's method was not only one of data and science—what the eighteenth century called erudition and reason—but also a matter of irony, again a complex, second-degree, reflexive perspective. That indirection is mostly absent from Hodgson, though we do find it throughout his work in a studied, distinctive form. I have in mind here the elaborate defamiliarization that words undergo as they become part of his thinking. Even more than with the transliterations from Arabic and other languages, every reader is struck by a venture that reinvents English, and adjectival nouns in particular: the technicalistic, the Oikoumeneic, the occidental, the agrarianate, the Islamicate, the citied, etcetera. These words were neither signs of a historian gone native, nor occasions for him to take a distance on his own history writing. They were tools in the service of objectivity. Under the pressure of a kind of positivism, his adjectives modified objects whose existence they continued to posit.

Yet I suspect Hodgson was deeply attuned to Gibbon's achievement specifically when it came to the subtleties of historical experience and understanding. This led both men to a less scientific, but I think richer and more characteristic sense of what a philosophic historian could be. In *Venture* too, that designation turns out to be important. It would have been easy enough for Hodgson to use the term casually, to refer to historians of the *faylasûf* tradition of writers, and so indeed we find a passing allusion to a tenth-century " 'philosophical' historian" (*Venture* 2:169). But Hodgson truly homes in on the term when he introduces Ibn-Khaldûn in the fourteenth century. The article makes the equation right in the title, "The Philosophical Historian: Ibn-Khaldûn," and shortly afterward it gives a possible explanation of why the term was valuable: "As a Faylasûf, Ibn-Khaldûn was concerned to work out a 'science' in the sense of a self-consistent body of demonstrable generalizations about historical change, generalizations which would in turn be based on premises taken from the demonstrated results of 'higher', i.e. more abstract, sciences—in this case chiefly biology, psychology, and geography" (*Venture* 2:478, 479–80; 3:119). I'm not sure that we recognize Gibbon or even Hodgson in every word of this admirable portrait, nor even that we should. I'm also not sure to what extent Gibbon recognized the existence of "higher" sciences than history, though he certainly felt that all sciences needed to be brought into communication with one another in the course of writing history.[12] But what strikes me as characteristic of both men is a Newtonian detail of this epistemology: the centrality of historical *change*. As Hodgson wrote of Ibn-Khaldûn several pages earlier, "In the Maghrib, if nowhere else, we see the unmistakeable decline in prosperity and power and cultural taste; and Ibn-Khaldûn was its great analyst, producing from it a major new departure in the scientific study of mankind" (*Venture* 2:476).

Ibn-Khaldûn's science was one of change. Gibbon too had singled out decline and fall as his epic subject, though he also posited the rise of other forces, including "barbarism and religion" (*Decline* 3:1068). I don't see any way to speak differently of Hodgson, whose concern for "florescence" and "creativity" in cultures is a major theme of *Venture*—especially when set against (1) the backdrop of Hodgson's unending inquiry into the conditions of decline of a major world civilization and (2) the powerful sense that his investigation into history took the form of a venture of all the sciences, something bold and risky at once. This is where the eighteenth- and twentieth-century philosophic historians perfectly agreed: in the central importance given not only to facts but to a culture's knowledge of itself, of reflexivity for historical beings and the need for historians to venture, if only to stumble, in a wide field. I take this to be the basis for Hodgson's insistence on the "citied" social order of Islam, as in a typical remark such as the following: "In particular, citied life implied an accelerated pace of historical change, of those actions and events that change the presuppositions of everyday life, to the point where the individual could become conscious of such change and of the possibilities of his own actions changing the life conditions of future generations" (*Venture* 1:109).

Gibbon too associates Islam, and change, with the development of cities, but also with historical actors in general, as here with the third-century emperor Decius in the heat of political crisis. He explains how Decius reinstated the office of censor in Roman life, but discourages us from considering that gesture as a matter of moralism: "At the same time when Decius was struggling with the violence of the tempest, his mind, calm and deliberate amidst the tumult of war, investigated the more general causes, that, since the age of the Antonines, had so impetuously urged the decline of the Roman greatness.

He soon discovered that it was impossible to replace that greatness on a permanent basis, without restoring public virtue, ancient principles and manners, and the oppressed majesty of the laws" (*Decline* 1:262). The emperor will of course fail to restore the empire's moral balance, but what must strike us here is the way that political dangers are connected to a consciously philosophical, historical, and political reading of reality. In the *Decline*, only a few emperors were "philosophic historians"; it didn't necessarily help to be one either. But they at least were capable of measuring how the public order was pitched to decline and fall. I suspect that this depth of vision also explains Gibbon's extensive treatment of Byzantium and the Eastern Empire that I mentioned earlier. His question was how and why social or political orders could continue to exist when apparently they had lost their dynamic force, and how such phenomena mattered to historical explanation—and to history. I trust you'll agree that this is a critical dimension of *Venture* as well, and implied by the work's subtitle: "Conscience and History in a World Civilization."

Language and Geography

In what follows, I'd like very briefly to evoke two other aspects of Gibbon's possible conversation with Marshall Hodgson. They are both linguistic and literary, in the broad sense of being both political and social as I defined them earlier. I suspect too that they bear a relation to what Hodgson describes as literary culture, *adab*, in Islamicate societies (e.g., *Venture* 1:239) and that Gibbon's world described as polite or polished societies. My first topic here involves the relation of foreign languages and geography; the second raises a question about "tone."

I spoke before of Hodgson's *stumbling* on world history, but that is clearly an exaggeration. Hodgson recognized in Islam a world civilization, perhaps even, in his day, the sturdiest and broadest of world civilizations (*Rethinking* 176). With his sense of Islam's geographical extent, its economic structure, and its cosmopolitan character, Hodgson was already verging on a conception of the world-historical, which he was tempted to call a "total civilization" (*Venture* 1:239) as well. In respect to Islam and to world history, it was Gibbon who was the more accidental figure, in the ways alluded to earlier. At any rate, what made Gibbon a significant historian and perhaps even a significant model for world historians was his ability to stumble on as well as to seize hold of a certain number of univalent meanings. Surely his early exposure to universal history seduced him by its epic dimensions rather than by the idea that here was one unified world. No doubt his youthful encounter with *The Arabian Nights* instructed him in "Oriental manners," but he also admitted that it delighted him as "fiction."[13] By far the most important aspect of Gibbon's relation to Islam involves a different kind of indirection. In 1752, at age fifteen, Gibbon was a student at Oxford hailing from a respectable-gentry background. The latter was not Quaker but Anglican Tory bordering on Jacobite. At any rate, he was intellectually unhappy and about to become unhappier still, even endangered. For at age fifteen he ventured to convert to Roman Catholicism, thereby breaking off from the Church of England and losing his legal right to study at Oxford. Very quickly this led to his being shipped off to Switzerland to be brought back to the Protestant faith, which he recovered even as he lost his native tongue for French. But before this confusing story had begun, there was a symptomatic episode that Gibbon later recalled in his autobiographical writings. He there remembers having had another idea of his life, as he walked with his tutor on a hill outside the town: "In our evening walks to the top of Heddington hill, we freely conversed on a variety of subjects. Since the days of Pocock and Hyde, Oriental learning has always been the pride of Oxford, and I once expressed an inclination to study Arabic. His prudence discouraged this childish fancy; but he neglected the fair occasion of directing the ardour of a curious mind" (*Autobiographies* 78–79). I do not wish to imply that the tutor's refusal to let Gibbon become an orientalist led to his doctrinal problems with Christianity. But the tutor's refusal was crucial for the history of historiography. It meant that if Gibbon remained interested in Middle Eastern and Central Asian cultures, which I think can be shown, he would be able to approach them only through a study of the West's interactions with them, and a knowledge of the Western languages that studied and sometimes translated their writings.[14] Even before going to Oxford, this specific curiosity had prompted Gibbon to begin to learn French, *not* so that he could read Voltaire's history of Louis XIV in the original but so that he could study the work of one of Louis XIV's greatest scholars, Barthélemy d'Herbelot de Molainville's great *Bibliothèque orientale* (1697).[15] French may have been the lingua franca of the eighteenth century, but it had its limits too. And English had not yet taken on the global importance it has today. As a result, if Gibbon was going to study the rise of Islam, it meant that he would need to mobilize the intellectual resources of Tacitus on the Germans as well as the Roman histories in order to come to grips with an upstart form of "republican" culture among the barbarians, delve into the West's relations with the Eastern Empire of Rome, and see how the Eastern Empire had negotiated its relations to Persia and Arabia. In other words, to approach the Middle East *without* Arabic, Gibbon would have to write the *Decline and Fall of the Roman Empire*, including both the western and eastern parts. Thus, it may not be altogether accurate to say that Gibbon wrote world history in order to discover and champion the identity of Europe. At least in its inception, his great work may have been an attempt to connect the larger world. Perhaps this is what he was discovering or rediscovering when at the end of his life he annotated his copy of the *Decline*.

The connection with an accomplished linguist like Hodgson is not obvious at first. However, we may understand Gibbon's significance in relation to remarks that appear in the opening section of *Venture*, where Hodgson criticizes "Arabistic and philologistic prejudices" (1:40–41). By the latter he meant the tendency to reduce all of Islamicate studies to one language exclusively, Arabic, and one cultural path—"the Cairene path" of Egypt, rather than through Ottoman or Persian sources. Gibbon's advantage here was that his spatial construction from Rome in the west to the New Rome in the east and beyond, replaced his intimate connection with one language and provided him with a general view of a considerable part of the Islamicate world. You might say this was a lucky accident. Even as it validates the sense that his history of the Muslims may well have been a serious achievement, it also helps to chart the fate of the *Decline*, which was standard reading for the high literary culture of nineteenth- and twentieth-century British imperialism. The *Decline* was a book that taught the new rulers of the world something about the space of the world. Perhaps unbeknownst to them, it did so by showing the interpenetration of forms of antiquity and modernity in contiguous parts of the world. Last, in this respect, Gibbon's "accident" may also speak to us today, in a world which is no longer one of rising imperialism but rather of populations in movement and shifting scales of understanding across the world. His example is concrete proof that historical method, reasoning, and precision—traits he derives in large part, I think, from Tacitus and Montesquieu—can still be a basis for studying foreign cultures in which one does not speak the language like that illusory standard, a native speaker. The requirement of full linguistic immersion is largely utopian, and it has to be of less value than spaces of intercultural dialogue, especially if the latter offers a more central role to that intercultural form par excellence, translation.

Tone in Gibbon and Hodgson

To reach my last subject, the question of tone, let me begin with an example that Gibbon cites toward the end of the *Decline* and that confirms some of the positions I've been alluding to. In the chapter on the Mongol invasion, he alludes in a note to a work whose title sounds a great deal like his own: "The History of the Growth and Decay (A.D. 1300–1683) of the Othman Empire was translated into English from the Latin MS. of Demetrius Cantemir, prince of Moldavia (London, 1734, in folio). The author is guilty of strange blunders in oriental history; but he was conversant with the language, the annals, and institutions of the Turks. . . . Yet I much doubt whether a partial and verbose compilation . . . can either instruct or amuse an enlightened age which requires from the historian some tincture of philosophy and criticism" (1:810n41). I have telescoped Gibbon's references to several works here, in order to underline how much critical acumen and philosophy mattered not only to the historian but also, rather bewilderingly, to an "enlightened" public. This helps to explain Gibbon's anxiety about whether the first volume of the *Decline* would please its readers, and it brings us to the question of tone, which we can now assume had to do with mixing philosophy and criticism, and being reflexive in the way a philosophic historian could. In his autobiographical writings, Gibbon recalled how hard it was to write the early chapters of the *Decline*: "The style of an author should be the image of his mind, but the choice and command of language is the fruit of exercise; many experiments were made before I could hit the middle tone between a dull Chronicle and a Rhetorical declamation; three times did I compose the first chapter, and twice the second and third, before I was tolerably satisfied with their effect" (*Autobiographies* 308). Once he had hit the tone, the *Decline* was off and running and, with some minor adjustments, it ran for three thousand pages. Gibbon had found a way to speak to his public, who bought, and read, him and apparently were satisfied in their demand for philosophical and critical instruction about who they were and where their world had come from. But here is the rub. At the time of the French Revolution, which was of course a nasty shock to him, Gibbon, an English émigré living in Switzerland, wrote in his autobiography that Britain had had historians, but that the French had not. "But if France, so rich in litterary [*sic*] merit, had produced a great original historian, his Genius would have formed and fixed the idiom to the proper tone, the peculiar mode of historical eloquence" (*Autobiographies* 278). This was not only insulting for a wide range of respected French historians. It was also an original interpretation of why French politics had been radicalized: the country had found no middle tone for understanding the relation of its past to its present. The past could look only like an imposture calling for upheaval. So all of its "social power"—to use an expression of Hodgson's[16]—was mustered against the available narratives of political order.

The connection with Hodgson is apparent enough. Sadly he did not live long enough to complete either *Venture* or "The Unity of World History." But we know he too wished to write for a distinctively multitiered audience—laymen, specialists, and "beginning students" (*Venture* 1:viii). The audience was diverse, and surely it has existed. But from Gibbon's standpoint, it may be that Hodgson became marginal and eccentric in language as in subject, where he would have been better off "becoming a classic." using the mainstream in language to educate an American and Western public to the character of a world it knew little about and hardly even imagined.[17] But Hodgson was not wrong either: he knew that the Tacitean-Montesquian synthesis was no longer satisfactory, and that world history could not simply be an extension of the kind of national or European cultural certainties that were the achievement of the Enlightenment. Perhaps, in that sense, he was even moving the English language, which has been the victor of the Great Transmutation, into a position of being both global and one language among others.

Notes

1. Edward Gibbon, *The History of the Decline and Fall of the Roman Empire*, 3 vols., ed. David Womersley (London: Allen Lane, 1994), 3:239 (hereafter cited in the text as *Decline*).

2. Gibbon continued to take "general history" seriously, and in the course of the *Decline* one encounters a small number of writers apparently working in that genre but almost always in relation to a delimited space. The powerful exception is perhaps Polybius. The confirmations include El-Tabari, "the Livy of the Arabians" (3:238n11), for Arabian history; Guicciardini for Italian; and Lorenz Mosheim for the Church.

3. Arnaldo Momigliano, "Edward Gibbon fuori e dentro la cultura italiana," in *Sesto contributo alla storia degli studi classici e del mondo antico* (Rome: Edizioni di Storia e Letteratura, 1980), 236. The passage translates: "In Byzantium Gibbon looked only for decadence and that is why he found only decadence. It is rather curious, because contradictory, that this decadence was static. This empire that never dies, or at least that survives its western twin by a thousand years, seems to resist all of Gibbon's witticisms. Younger Byzantinists who strike off in the opposite direction in search of the vitality of Byzantium are Gibbon's harshest critics" (my translation).

4. Steven Runciman, "Gibbon and Byzantium," in "Edward Gibbon and the Decline and Fall of the Roman Empire," *Daedalus* 105, no. 3 (Summer 1976): 103–10.

5. Marshall G. S. Hodgson, *The Venture of Islam: Conscience and History in a World Civilization* (Chicago: University of Chicago Press, 1974), 1:240 (hereafter cited in the text as *Venture*); the phrasing here tells us that Hodgson favored two or three centuries.

6. Samuel Johnson, *A Dictionary of the English Language* (1755; abridged 1756), reprinted and edited by Alexander Chalmers, 1843 (London: Studio Editions, 1994).

7. Cf. the financial conditions obtained by William Robertson for his *History of the Reign of Charles V* (1769).

8. Which is to say, several times in *Venture* and again in the chapters reproduced by E. Burke III from the volume Hodgson did not live to complete on world history. I have not had the occasion to study the considerable Hodgson archives.

9. Marshall G. S. Hodgson, "The Objectivity of Large-Scale Historical Inquiry," in *Rethinking World History: Essays on Europe, Islam, and World History*, ed. Edmund Burke III (Cambridge: Cambridge University Press, 1993), 265 (hereafter this volume is cited in the text as *Rethinking*).

10. At least in part: another dimension is related to nineteenth-century German philosophy of history, which we hear in absentia whenever Hodgson speaks of civilizations as "world-historical" (e.g., *Venture*, 1:96).

11. The 1791 revisions that Gibbon made in his own copy of the *Decline* may be found in 3:1093ff.

12. Robert Mankin, "Incorporer la science: Le cas d'Edward Gibbon," *Dix-huitième siècle* 40 (2008): 121–37.

13. Among his youthful pleasures in reading, he records: "I soon tasted the Arabian nights entertainments—a book of all ages, since in my present maturity I can revolve without contempt that pleasing medley of Oriental manners and supernatural fictions." *The Autobiographies of Edward Gibbon*, ed. John Murray (London: John Murray, 1896), 118 (hereafter cited in the text as *Autobiographies*). Cf. Hodgson's allusion to the *Thousand and One Nights* as describing "the social patterns" when a "political minimum" of collective organization was reached (*Venture*, 2:69).

14. I have developed this argument in the opening section of my "Edward Gibbon: Historian in Space," in *A Companion to Enlightenment Historiography*, ed. Sophie Bourgault and Robert Sparling (Leiden: Brill, 2013), 29–31.

15. *Autobiographies*, 58. See also *Decline*, 3:541n41.

16. See, for instance, the first essay in *Rethinking*.

17. "Since our concern was speech, and speech impelled us / To purify the dialect of the tribe / And urge the mind to aftersight and foresight"; T. S. Eliot, "Little Gidding," in *Four Quartets*, 10th printing (London: Faber & Faber, 1955).

CHAPTER FOUR

Hodgson, Islam, and World History in the Modern Age

Christopher A. Bayly

Marshall G. S. Hodgson was one of the founding figures of the writing of modern world history and a critical influence on the development of the Western understanding of Islam. He was what might be called a counter-orientalist, in that he used the tools of oriental scholarship to create a new and more empathetic understanding of the Muslim world. Unlike his now more contentious successor, Edward Said, he worked directly on the cultural heritage of Islam, while Said could broadly be said to be an intellectual historian of Europe. Hodgson's central argument was essentially, to adapt Dipesh Chakrabarty's phrase, that across much of historical record, Europe must be "provincialized." There was no teleology of progress linking classical Greece and Rome, the Renaissance, the Enlightenment, and the global expansion of Europe. Instead, from the seventh to the seventeenth century at least, it was Islam that represented humanistic civilization through much of the world. By linking East and South Asia to Europe, Muslims disseminated many of the key developments in the arts, literature, and science through Eurasia and Africa, while consistently emphasizing the importance of individual conscience, spiritual uplift, and the endurance of civilization.

Yet Edmund Burke III, one of Hodgson's admirers and the editor of his posthumous collection of essays, *Rethinking World History* (1993), writes of his major work, *The Venture of Islam*, that, in some respects, it was "a splendid anachronism," promoting a quasi-idealist approach to a subject which had also to be understood to a great extent through a consideration of demographic, economic, and social change.[1] Other historians have argued that Hodgson merely succeeded in replacing Islamocentrism for Eurocentrism, both approaches that underestimate the differences within broad civilizations and also the interactions between them. While other chapters in the volume consider

Hodgson's background in Chicago, American historiography, and the earlier history of Islam, this chapter is particularly concerned with Hodgson's career as a modern world historian and his relationship to European thought and departures from it.

Hodgson in World Context

At this wider level, Hodgson and some of his contemporaries drew on and transformed into an American form of thought the works of a number of Continental European writers on Islam and world history. While Hegel, in particular, had held that India was an immature civilization, distorted by Hindu aestheticism, he had viewed early Islamic monotheism much more favorably, as one stage in the onward march of the spirit of freedom. Only later did Islam, according to Hegel, "retreat into oriental ease and repose," with the result that the single truly free person in Muslim societies was the ruler. Arguably, one can trace a late version of this understanding of Islam as the embodiment of the spirit of freedom in Hodgson's own work. Hodgson, however, insisted that Islam's retreat did not truly occur until the eighteenth century (*Venture* 3:134).

By 1914, several positive and comparative views of Islam and Asia had already come to the fore, especially those of Continental European scholarship, and these influenced Hodgson. They ranged from Nietzsche's characterization of the Prophet as a hero (anticipated by Carlyle) to Weber's theorizing of the relationship between religion and rationalization in world context. As Burke again notes, the French Arabist Louis Massignon and the Austrian American Islamist Gustave von Grunebaum were particularly influential for the development of Hodgson's thought. What were the resonances of these thinkers for him?

Louis Massignon's writing can be understood partly as a response to the dilemmas of French colonialism in Algeria.[2] Massignon had relations among colonial officials in the colony, which he visited in 1901–2 following his graduation from the lycée Louis le Grand in Paris. Later, during a perilous visit to Mesopotamia in 1907, he emerged as a reconvert to Catholic Christianity, but one deeply influenced by Islamic humanism. Belief followed from "the visitation of a stranger," meaning God, to the individual spirit. As a Christian mystic in a Muslim context, he was also inspired by the French Algerian hermit Charles de Foucauld, who had become a kind of St. Francis to the Twareg tribes of North Africa. Massignon's *La passion de Hussayn Ibn Mansur al-Hallaj*, dealing with the great ninth-century mystical scholar, brought these two religious strains together.[3] His deep concern with mysticism was later criticized by Said, who, while generally exonerating him from his own version of malign orientalism, believed that Massignon had marginalized the legalistic and social dimension of Islam. Yet this obsession was what gave Massignon a unique empathy with Muslims across the world.

Apart from Massignon's scholarly range and imagination, his attraction for Hodgson lay in his Christian religious commitment and his deep love of the Sufi tradition. For Massignon, the inner, mystical dimension of Islam resonated with his love for the spiritualism of saints such as Teresa of Avila. It is true, of course, that Hodgson himself was aware of, and ambivalent about the intellectual dangers of reading Islam out of Christianity or vice versa. Yet his own Quaker beliefs, which held that God exists in everyone, certainly predisposed him to a version of Sufism disciplined by the reason of the *ulama*. This was a position closer perhaps to the early scholarship of the North Indian *madrasah* of Deoband and unlike the more rigid Arabian Wahhabism. The compassion of the Sufi provided an entrée for Massignon into the world of universalistic humanism and equality which he imagined. Ritual and theology were downplayed in both traditions. Indeed, for some Quakers, Christ was an exemplary figure, a prophet rather than a divine being. A secondary feature linking Massignon and Hodgson was their determination to include Persian thought and literature in their studies of the Islamic world, which they felt had been dominated overmuch by the experience of the Arabs. Mansur al-Hallaj himself was born in the province of Fars in Persia and his family had originally been Zoroastrian.

Yet it is also important to be aware of the differences between the sensibility of Hodgson and that of Massignon. Hodgson had flourished in a university which was acutely conscious of the rising power of the United States in the world and a teaching tradition designed to equip the citizens of the new superpower with regional knowledge and sympathy for oppressed peoples. Hodgson may have seen his "history of conscience" and his global ecumene as an implicit rejection of the hostilities of the Cold War. Yet he was also aware, in his later years at least, of the force of the Islamic revival which was reflected in the rise of the economic power of the oil-rich Arabs, the foundation of Pakistan, the influence of the Muslim Brotherhood, and the like. The last chapters of the third volume of *Venture* record Hodgson's ambivalence toward, but also his admiration for, these new forces (3:411–41).

By contrast, Massignon, who was much older than Hodgson and even more devoted to mysticism than he was, struck a note of nostalgia and regret for the decline of classical Islam in his works. History for Massignon was an essential component of "the art of compassion." The collection *L'Islam et l'Occident* (1947), which Massignon edited with Cheik Abd el Razek of the al-Azhar Muslim University of Cairo, begins with an essay by Jean Ballard.[4] This bewailed the decline of both Islam and the West, the latter corrupted by Fascism, Communism, and genocidal war. Massignon himself, writing after a visit to Herat, pictured Islam crushed between a declining British Empire to the south and an aggressive Communist power to the north. Worse still was "*le choc morale des techniques européennes*,"[5] perhaps a forerunner of Hodgson's rather disparaging notion of Western "technicalism," Euro-American with material as opposed to moral change. Massignon awaited "*le renaissance, le classicisme arabe nouveau qui mettra l'Islam de niveau avec les cimes de la culture mondiale*."[6] But this was still wanting in the 1940s, just as Catholic Christianity was embattled in his native France. Despite this subtle difference in sensibilities, however, there is no doubting the influence of Massignon and his French coworkers on Hodgson. For instance, the essay by Emile Dermenghem in *L'Islam et l'Occident*, "Temoignage de l'Islam," marks Islam out as "*un nation intermediare*" helping to link Europe, East Asia, and black Africa.[7] This again is a clear precursor to Hodgson's idea of an Afro-Eurasian ecumene.

The stance of Gustave von Grunebaum, a direct colleague of Hodgson as a professor of Arabic in Chicago, was attractive to Hodgson for similar reasons. A refugee from the cosmopolitan world of the late Austro-Hungarian Empire, von Grunebaum left Europe as it was engulfed by the Nazis. He was convinced of the "intellectual obligation resting on the Western student of Islam" to interpret it humanely to his own society for its particular "moral worth."[8] This was a position which Hodgson warmly endorsed, though von Grunebaum's passion was to explain this worth through a detailed textual study of Arabic poetry. His *Medieval Islam* achieved a similar synthetic scope to Hodgson's, though for a more limited time period, as it attempted to reveal the universal humanity of Islamic civilization through Arabic literature. Von Grunebaum and the South Asian scholar Aziz Ahmad worked together on the Muslims of India and Pakistan during Hodgson's final years.[9] It seems likely that this "shift to the East" provides one context for Hodgson's own engagement with South Asian historiography, which only came quite late in his life and informs the final chapters of volume 3 of *Venture*.

Finally, although he did not read Russian, Hodgson took note of the work of Russian and Soviet Islamists, particularly Vasily Bartold, who had also worked to shift historians' attention away from Europe and anticipated Hodgson's arguments at several points. He argued, for instance, that Persian culture was as significant as Arabic in the development of Islam and that Muslim society and scientific expertise did not die out in the fifteenth century. He specifically noted that "achievements in technique do not by themselves lead to progress in social life,"[10] prefiguring Hodgson's later downplaying of European technical developments in the early modern period. Bartold also generally downplayed the idea of despotism, pointing to Muslim city life and corporate social activity. The implication that in many respects Muslim society at its peak prefigured Communism with organized civil society directed by strong leadership must have pleased the Soviet censors.

Few British scholars of Islam—or, for that matter, "Ivy League" American scholars—appear either as colleagues of Hodgson or in his footnotes. One of the few was Hamilton Gibb, another student of Arabic literature and society, who wrote *Mohammedanism: An Historical Survey* (1949).[11] Hodgson would have approved Gibb's point of religious departure as a Scottish Protestant who admired the democratic spirit of Islam. But he would have objected to other aspects of his writing. Gibb still wrote in a Social Darwinist tradition that saw civilizations rise and fall like living organisms. He asserted the superiority of Christianity to Islam in a way that Hodgson never did. Unlike Massignon and Hodgson, Gibb tended to marginalize Sufism, Shiʿism, and even Arab scientific rationality. Finally, Gibb and his coworker, Bowen, believed that many of the most creative features of early modern Islam were consequences of the influence of Christian-convert servants of the Ottoman regime who originated in eastern Europe. This reflected a subtle version of that Eurocentrism which was Hodgson's main target throughout his life.

Hodgson's Context in Transnational Historiography

Reading Hodgson's collected essays one might get the impression that he was one of the few voices crying out in the wilderness against the disparagement of Islam and the espousal of a Eurocentric version of world history. In fact, the situation was much more complex. From the middle of the nineteenth century there were many historians and social commentators who took issue with the organicism and progressive historicism which saw Europe emerging from classical antiquity through the Renaissance to stand at the pinnacle of human achievement. This critical historiography, as in Hodgson's case, was often tinged with religious sentiment. In particular, many such writers, not only on Islam but also on India and China, displayed what could be called a redemptive turn of mind. They believed that Asia's contemporary humiliations could be redeemed by emphasizing those aspects of its religion and culture which had once put them at the pole of human achievement. Yet it was not only Asians who needed to be redeemed. For Western imperialism had wrought disaster across the world and could be atoned for only by humility, scholarship, and education.

True, the dominant liberal imperialists of the late Victorian era despised Islamic society and the Ottoman Empire in particular or argued that their social and political structures were primitive. This theme was particularly blatant in the writing of Henry Maine, James Bryce, and William Gladstone, the longtime British prime minister himself. Hodgson later dismissed Arnold Toynbee, not only because of the alleged naïveté of his understanding of the nature of civilizations,[12] but also because he fell squarely into this tradition of writing off Islam as tyrannical and the Ottoman government as a mere assemblage of tribute takers. Yet even in Britain, there was another radical liberal school which viewed Islam and Asian societies in a more positive light. Thomas W. Arnold, for instance, attacked the views of William Muir and other Indian colonial officials who derided Islam as a religion of blood and conquest, cemented by "the love of rapine and the lust of spoil."

Arnold, who had taught at the modernist Anglo-Muhammadan College at Aligarh in North India, stressed the peaceful expansion of the faith and its appeal to slaves and the underprivileged. He protested against the "prejudice and unfairness" of ignoring the "missionary work" of Islam, anticipating Hodgson.[13] Like Hodgson and Massignon, he was attracted to the hermetic religious life, translating the *Little Flowers of St Francis*. Again, like the later Chicago school, he was aware of French, German, and Dutch scholarship, pointing to the work of the Paris journal *Revue du monde musulman*, which took an enlightened view of the political stirrings in the Muslim world after 1900 such as the Persian revolution of 1903. Another British scholar, E. G. Browne, took a similarly benign view of Iran's emergence from monarchical despotism, again drawing on contemporary French work.[14] Later, in the 1930s, Joseph Needham, a pupil of Browne and an Anglican Christian and historian of science, wrote of the origin of Western knowledge in China and envisioned history as a story of the survival of the most altruistic, not of the genetically fittest.[15]

Hodgson himself sought to reorient world history away from its Western axis by treating Europe as a "cape" or "promontory" on the margins of an Afro-Eurasian ecumene. Yet this effort had begun nearly a century before in India, a country which is more often alluded to in passing rather than discussed in Hodgson's early essays on global history. In the 1820s, Rammohan Roy and

Ram Raz had both critiqued the European view that representative government had emerged only in Greece, citing the ancient Indian deliberative body the *panchayat*.[16] Ram Raz also refuted the view that Indian architecture was derived from Greek or Egyptian models. Fifty years later, K. T. Telang demolished the notion that the great Hindu epic the Ramayana was derivative of the Greek myths. By 1900 Aurobindo Ghose and the young Mahatma Gandhi were asserting that European civilization was morally inferior to those of Asia, excelling only in what Hodgson later called "technicalism." Okakura Kakuzo's *Ideals of the East* (1904) sparked off a whole series of works on the superiority of Asian art and culture. Notable here was Ananda Kentish Coomaraswamy, the Anglo-Ceylonese art historian who worked in Princeton University for much of Hodgson's own lifetime.

It is, in fact, quite puzzling that, at least in his world history essays, Hodgson paid so little attention to non-European writers who by the 1930s and 1940s had flooded English and French literature with books and articles attempting to rectify the Eurocentric bias he deplored. His focus, of course, continued to be on Islamic society in these general essays. But even in western Asia and North Africa, a figure such as Salama Musa, the Coptic essayist and violent critic of British dominion in his country, was an antiorientalist who anticipated Said both in rhetoric and argument.[17] In West Africa, Dr. J. B. Danquah attacked the distorting effects of the modern West, which had betrayed its original Christian ideals.

Many of these authors, European, Asian, and African, could be seen as religious reformers and even mystics in their different traditions. Not all of them were in any sense modernizers. Many of them deeply deplored "technicalization," falling back on ideas of the simple morality of the East as in the case of Gandhi or Kakuzo. Others, such as T. E. Lawrence, Massignon, and de Foucauld, were entranced, not by the modernism of the Tanzimat, the Ottoman, and later Turkish reformers, but the simple life of the Bedu, and gloried in young male Arab manhood. A particularly up-front version of this homoerotic religiosity in the Indian case was Edward Carpenter, a British gay radical who supported Indian nationalism and believed that the *lingams* (stylized representations of male sexual organs) found in some Hindu temples were a premonition of worldwide sexual liberation.

Hodgson's Posthumous Influence—or Lack of It

Setting Hodgson's work in its period, one of continuing Western dominance and late idealist thought, makes it clear why discussion of his work dwindled in quantity and quality within a few years of his death. The profession turned away sharply from the idealism of Massignon and even Hodgson's more restrained call to write "public and morally aware history" seemed at odds with academic hyperprofessionalism. In English-language historiography, Herbert Butterfield was perhaps the last major writer to make his religious confession so clear in his work. Albert Hourani wrote luminously about Arabic thought, but the tone of Islamic historiography in Britain was captured by the two-volume *Cambridge History of Islam* (1971), a massive compilation of detailed empirical narratives, largely devoid of reflection, argument, or theory.

The decline of idealism was, however, combined with what Hodgson might well have considered a form of historians' "technicalism." Even the disagreements with William McNeill on the timing of the Western breakout from the ecumene and rise to dominance seemed marginal compared with the turn toward the history of demography, capitalism, and economic change which overtook the field of world history after 1970. The background of this shift can be found in two bodies of writing. First, there was the rearmament of Marxism in Continental Europe and Britain signaled by the appearance of works such as those by the sadly departed Eric Hobsbawm, Andre Gunder Frank, Perry Anderson, and, rather later, Michael Hardt and Antonio Negri. All these reflected a sophisticated superstructural interpretation of world history, yet paid considerably more attention to factors and modes of production than Hodgson had ever done. Parallel with this work was a range of publications which could be classified as non-Marxist materialist in character. Here the looming figure was Fernand Braudel, who finally dispelled the French version of idealist historiography represented by Massignon and propelled the Annales School to the center of historical scholarship.

A direct intellectual descendant of Braudel was K. N. Chaudhuri, who wrote on world history and the history of the "Islamicate" world—to use Hodgson's term—from the bottom up. It is noteworthy that in Chaudhuri's most general work, *Asia before Europe*,[18] one which dwells on temporality and the geography of a large part of Afro-Eurasia, Hodgson does not merit a single footnote, mention in the text, or entry in the bibliography. This is in sharp contrast to Chaudhuri's near-deification of Braudel. Hodgson is also absent in Chris Wickham's study, *Framing the Early Middle Ages*, which brings together the Islamicate and the Christian Mediterranean worlds as Hodgson had done in volume 2 of *Venture*, though concentrating on aristocracies, peasantries, rural settlements, and exchange. The works published or edited by A. G. Hopkins on the history of "globalization" once again generally neglect

Hodgson.[19] Hopkins and his contributors emphasize trade and exchange and insofar as they consider the Islamic world, it is almost exclusively as an economic area.

Recently, several younger historians have turned to the issue which Hodgson debated with McNeill: the tipping point when "Europe" achieved its key economic and political advantage over the rest of the world. Kenneth Pomeranz wrote of the Great Divergence, between Europe and China, dating it very late, toward the end of the eighteenth century when Britain finally achieved maritime dominance and the beginnings of industrialization.[20] R. Bin Wong wrote *China Transformed: Historical Change and the Limits of European Experience*. His newer book, *Before and Beyond Divergence* (2011),[21] coauthored with Jean Laurent Rosenthal, extends the analysis of comparative European and Chinese political economy. The strength of this work is its very careful approach to comparative methodology. Rather than arguing that China and Europe took fundamentally different paths to modernity and industrialization, Bin Wong and Rosenthal illustrate a good deal of commonality between aspects of the Chinese political economy and its European counterpart. In doing so, they emphasize issues of scale and the way in which relatively small differences (e.g., in the form of property rights, etc.) had significant longer-term consequences through to the present. What is most impressive about this work is the fact that it refuses to make grandiose historical claims about "Chinese exceptionalism" or, conversely, simply to absorb European into Chinese historical paradigms, or vice versa. Finally, Prasannan Parthasarathi has brought India back into the debate about "the expansion of Europe" in his *Why Europe Grew Rich and Asia Did Not* (2011). Here again in these works Hodgson's own legacy is missing while what he called technicalism receives consistent emphasis.

Historians' own recent technicalism has not necessarily, however, completely refuted Hodgson's arguments of the 1950s and 1960s. The spirited debate with McNeill about the voyages of discovery and the European "breakout" should be seen as a draw. Hodgson was right that the Islamicate world remained the dominant agrarian civilization well into the seventeenth century, continuing to expand on its Mediterranean and South Asian frontiers. Yet McNeill had not committed a "disastrous mistake." Hodgson was too quick to write off the transformative consequences of the European invasion of the New World. The discovery of silver not only wholly reoriented the world economy, but the forms of governance and conversion developed there were already being spread to Asia and Africa by the end of the sixteenth century.

Burke pointed to the apparent contradiction between Hodgson's acceptance of rapid European technical development in the eighteenth century and his assertion that this was a global phenomenon. In fact, Jan de Vries's concept of industrious revolutions which preceded the industrial revolution can probably be extended to developments in silk and cotton production in the Chinese, South Asian, and Ottoman-Arab worlds. This argument need not detract from the significance of British industrialization or the concomitant revolutions in European thought and social organization which Hodgson did indeed unduly diminish with his overemphasis on technicalization. Again, scholarship since the 1970s has reinforced his view that the eighteenth century was the low point of the political fortune of the Islamic world. Yet at the same time, significant intellectual and social movements were in train which pointed to long-term revival. These included the development of the Urdu language, the emergence of schools of thought in Cairo and Delhi which confronted the problem of reconciling Islam and modernity and latterly the modernized army and statecraft of Mehmet Ali in Egypt and the Tanzimat reforms across the empire.

Hodgson's Legacy Today

So is Hodgson's writing an anachronism? I am struck by the fact that, while he rarely appears in footnotes, so many Asian and world historians I have spoken to in the last few years continue to express admiration for him and urge their students to read him. It is almost as if at some unconscious level, historians mourn the purging of moral judgment and idealism from their subject. History should be "philosophy teaching by example" once again.

Hodgson's conclusion to the final chapter of *The Venture of Islam* might seem on the face of it a softer anticipation of Huntington's *The Clash of Civilizations*. Here he ponders the incompatibilities between Western technicalism and democracy and Islamicate traditionalism and also reflects on conflicts between Muslims, Christians, and Jews. Yet his approach is actually much more subtle than this. He argues for the common "conscience-mindedness" of all world civilizations and their essential humanism. The formerly Christian world, because of its wealth and power, had the leisure and possibilities of reflection, he implies, to move away from the most mechanical features of technicalization and stress the individual conscience once again. The position was more difficult in Islam, because of the overwhelming need for change in the face of poverty, lack of resources, and overpopulation. This resulted in a resort to an excessively legalized form of sharia-mindedness and a rigid interpretation of history and tradition, which, in turn frustrated efforts to accommodate modernity without abandoning faith.

Many contemporary observers would appreciate the continuing relevance of this interpretation. Even if parts of the Arab world have dramatically improved their standards of living, the preponderance of poor, uneducated young men in Muslim populations across the world and the continuing presence of Western neo-imperialism in the form of drone attacks, bombing, or outright military intervention have not greatly changed the picture which Hodgson painted in the early 1960s. The result has been an even greater emphasis by some Muslim elites and governments on rigid Salafi neo-traditionalist doctrines or their Shiʿite equivalents. It is easy enough to point to the Taleban or the transnational influence of al-Qaeda or "Isil," but there has been a much wider move afoot in Muslim countries toward more rigid forms of sharia-mindedness and a distancing from individualistic styles of thought and practice, Sufi or otherwise. This has resulted from the desire of authoritarian governments to buttress their legitimacy as much as from the wealth of Wahhabi Arabia and the Gulf states. Even semidemocratic explosions seen in Iran in the 1970s or in the "Arab spring" of 2011 have often propelled relatively conservative Islamic forces into power, whether they were the ayatollahs in the late 1970s, or the Muslim Brotherhood or the Tablighi Jamaat more recently.

Sufism in particular has tended to be marginalized in the continuation of a process which Hodgson observed with concern in the 1960s and which could be traced back to the rise of Ibn Saud in the 1920s. We can take the case of the great South and Southeast Asian network of Nagore Dargahs, the network of Sufi shrines across India.[22] Whereas the custodians of the Indian mother shrine thirty years ago emphasized the merging of Hindu and Muslim notions of the divine, as embodied in the life of the Nagore "saint," today's descendants have tended to sever themselves from any Hindu inheritance. Meanwhile in Singapore, the local Nagore Dargah has been converted into a museum of Islamic history with scarcely a mention of its original Sufi role. In Pakistan, the powerful Jamaat parties have been equally hostile to the Sufi traditions of parts of the population, though their ire and exclusionism have more often been directed against Ahmadiyyas, Christians, and most recently Shiʿites.

Equally, this conflict between Islamist conservatism and other religions, which Hodgson lamented in the case of Jews and Arabs in Palestine in his own day, has increased in violence in Palestine, but also in the Sudan, in West Africa, Burma, and Thailand. One of the most arresting aspects of this process has been what might be called the Islamization of other faith groups. V. D. Savarkar, ideologue of Hindutva ("Hinduness"), appropriated a vulgarized notion of Islamization in his version of a Hindu realm expanding through violence. Similarly, Christians in parts of Africa have adopted attitudes superficially representative of Muslims in their campaigns against sexual diversity. Hodgson traced the origins of religious conflict back to the rigidification of the *millet* system under eighteenth-century Ottoman rule, followed by the exclusion of Christians, Jews, and Armenians from the armies of the nineteenth-century Tanzimat period. European divide-and-rule policies in Lebanon or Iraq consolidated these conflicts in the early twentieth century, he argued. Implicitly, authoritarian postcolonial rulers—Musharaf, the Assads, Gaddafi, for instance—perpetuated this system to stay in power, though Hodgson only saw the beginning of this pattern in his lifetime. Even today's supposedly democratic revolutions appear to be promoting a popularization of religious conflict as much as an empowerment of the citizen, as witness the recent battles between Coptic Christians, Muslim brotherhood supporters, and pious military leaders in Egypt.

Not all interpretations of recent events follow the more gloomy reflections in Hodgson's final chapters, though. Some seem to suggest the more hopeful outcomes, which are also set out in what were, after all, posthumously published notes. The reactive and narrow form of Salafi sharia-mindedness which he so much regretted has clearly captured the attention of scholars and the media in the decade since 9/11 and this has reflected back on historical study. But a quieter, more individualistic form of public belief, which is compatible with modern democratic forms, has by no means disappeared from the Muslim world. Mahomed Mahathir of Malaysia, for instance, became the bane of the Western media. But his anti-Western bias may well have been a shield to cover a much more positive campaign to create a modern form of Muslim citizenship within this religiously plural society. In Thailand purist forms of Islam have gained in strength but are by no means predominant across the country.[23] Again, in Indonesia, occasional Islamist atrocities should not obscure the fact that an admittedly flawed form of democracy has come into being. Indian Muslims for their part have broadly participated in the country's forms of representational government and have apparently been immunized against extremism. Recent outrages, such as the Mumbai killings of 2006, originated in the Indian government's suppression of dissent in Kashmir, not in a general turn toward violent Islamism. Even under the Recep Erdogan government, a reasonable balance between official secularism and Islamic revivalism persisted in Turkey, at least until 2013. Most striking, in areas close to the Taleban insurgency and far beyond, more inclusive forms of Muslim society have continued to flourish, as Magnus Marsden's studies of Chitral and adjacent areas of the Pakistani Punjab have demonstrated.[24]

The diaspora of Muslims to Western countries has also helped keep alive a strong and balanced tradition of Muslim scholarship on Islamic history, which has fed back into Middle Eastern and South and Southeast Asian institutions such as the American universities in Cairo and Beirut and Jamia Millia Islamiya in India. In economic life, Charles Tripp has recently documented the many ways in which Muslims have managed or appropriated aspects of Western technicalism and capitalism.[25] Finally, one could draw attention to the civil society activism of Muslim women in many parts of the world, in opposition to extreme Wahhabism, Taleban-ization, and other forms of patriarchal purism.[26] Hodgson wrote very little about women or issues of gender. That historiographical revolution was only just beginning at the time of his death. But he would doubtless have understood its importance for his history of individual conscience.

Despite, the internal conflicts within Hodgson's interpretation of world history, current events have also tended to confirm his view that historical change, for most of human history, has to be understood as a pattern of adaptation across the whole Afro-Eurasian ecumene. Works such as Ricardo Duchesne's *The Uniqueness of Western Civilization* (2011) continue to appear,[27] but their tone is a little more self-aware than the Eurocentric and Westernist teleologies of the 1940s and 1950s which Hodgson deplored. In a minor way, indeed, the emergence of the television station Aljazeera has decisively displaced Mercator's worldview, centering its maps and its programs on the Muslim world. More ominously, perhaps, China's recent discussion about whether to bail out the eurozone economies by buying infrastructure and its massive financial hold in the United States and Africa have evidently tipped the world away from the West. Meanwhile, Indian homegrown technicalism has been on show in Bangalore, while Indian businessmen now figure among the ten richest people in the world for the first time since about 1720. Truly, Europe has once again begun to retreat to its status as a cape or promontory of Afro-Eurasia, as it was for Hodgson when he wrote *The Venture of Islam* and pondered on the course of world history a generation ago.

Other schools of world-historical writing have taken up Hodgson's challenge. The Indian subaltern studies school which represents the history of the underprivileged has found its converts as far away as Latin America. Even if these writers have tended to homogenize the experience and resistance of the poor peasants and workers, this has been a critical intervention in world history writing. A leading exponent, Dipesh Chakrabarty, wishes to "provincialize" Europe. By this he does not mean ignore or attack it, but he emphasizes the need to show how European ideas were appropriated, transformed, and used in other contexts.[28] Equally, challenging Eurocentrism does not mean insisting on a seamlessly connected world history in which power and historical ruptures are played down. Indian democracy, for instance, is profoundly different from Western democracy and probably owes little to the minor advances in group representation which British colonialism introduced there. What we need to do is to be aware: be aware of the global context of change; be aware of the historiography of other parts of the world; and be aware of how across much of world history Europe itself was partly formed beyond its geographical limits, as Marshall G. S. Hodgson always insisted.

Notes

1. Marshall G. S. Hodgson, *Rethinking World History: Essays on Europe, Islam, and World History*, ed. Edmund Burke III (Cambridge: Cambridge University Press, 1993); Hodgson, *The Venture of Islam: Conscience and History in a World Civilization*, 3 vols. (Chicago: University of Chicago Press, 1974) (hereafter cited in the text as *Venture*).

2. For Massignon, see Mary Louise Gude, *Louis Massignon: The Crucible of Compassion* (Notre Dame, IN: University of Notre Dame Press, 1996).

3. Cf. L. Massignon, *Akhbar al Hallaj: Texte ancien relatif à la prédication et au supplice du mystique musulman* (Paris: Larose, 1936).

4. Jean Ballard, introduction to L. Massignon, Cheik Abd El Razek, and Carlo Suarès, eds., *L'Islam et l'Occident* (Paris: Cahiers du Sud, 1947).

5. L. Massignon, "Situation internationale de l'Islam," in *L'Islam et l'Occident*, 14.

6. Ibid.

7. Ibid., 386.

8. Franz Rosenthal, "In memoriam: Gustave E. von Grunebaum, 1909–72," *International Journal of Middle East Studies* 4 (1973): 357.

9. Aziz Ahmad and G. E. von Grunebaum, eds., *Muslim Self-Statement in India and Pakistan, 1857–1968* (Wiesbaden: Harrassowitz, 1970). For a major later study of Islam in India, see Andre Wink, *Al-Hind: The Making of the Indo-Islamic World*, vol. 1, *Early Medieval India and the Expansion of Islam, 7th–11th Centuries* (Leiden: Brill, 1990), and later volumes.

10. Vasily V. Bartold [Wilhelm Barthold], *Mussulman Culture*, trans. Shahid Suhrawardy (Calcutta: University of Calcutta, 1934), 135.

11. I have discussed Gibb in "The Orient," in *History and Historians in the Twentieth Century*, ed. Peter Burke (Oxford: Oxford University Press, 1998), 97–98; see also Anne K. S.

Lambton, "Sir Hamilton Gibb, 1895–1971," *Bulletin of the School of Oriental and African Studies* 35, no. 2 (1972): 338–45.

12. Hodgson, "The Interrelations of Societies in History," in *Rethinking*, 12.

13. Bayly, "The Orient," in *History and Historians*, ed. Burke, 99.

14. E. G. Browne, *The Persian Revolution 1905–1909* (Cambridge: Cambridge University Press, 1910).

15. Joseph Needham et al., *Science and Civilisation in China*, 27 vols. (Cambridge: Cambridge University Press 1954–2008).

16. The issue of the "ancient Indian constitution" is discussed in C. A. Bayly, *Recovering Liberties: Indian Thought in the Age of Liberalism and Empire* (Cambridge: Cambridge University Press, 2011), 42–73.

17. Salama Musa, *The Education of Salama Musa*, trans. L. O. Schuman (Leiden: Brill, 1961).

18. K. N. Chaudhuri, *Asia before Europe* (Cambridge: Cambridge University Press, 1990).

19. Though I am glad to say that I do mention him in an essay in A. G. Hopkins's *Globalization in World History* (London: Pimlico, 2002), 63!

20. Kenneth Pomeranz, *The Great Divergence: Europe, China, and the Making of the Modern World Economy* (Princeton, NJ: Princeton University Press, 2000).

21. Jean-Laurent Rosenthal and R. Bin Wong, *Before and Beyond Divergence: The Politics of Economic Change in China and Europe* (Cambridge, MA: Harvard University Press, 2011).

22. Susan Bayly, *Saints, Goddesses and Kings: Hindus, Muslims and Christians in South India* (Cambridge: Cambridge University Press, 1993).

23. Rajeswary Ampalavanar Brown, *Islam in Modern Thailand: Faith, Philanthropy and Politics* (London: Routledge, 2014), esp. 41–81.

24. Magnus Marsden, *Living Islam: Muslim Religious Experience in Pakistan's North West Frontier* (Cambridge: Cambridge University Press, 2005).

25. Charles Tripp, *Islam and the Moral Economy: The Challenge of Capitalism* (Cambridge: Cambridge University Press, 2006).

26. For example, Ghada Hashem Talhami, *The Mobilization of Muslim Women in Egypt* (Gainesville: University Press of Florida, 1996); Shahida Lateef, *Muslim Women in India: Political and Private Realities 1890s–1980s* (New Delhi: Kali for Women, 1990).

27. See, e.g., Ricardo Duchesne, *The Uniqueness of Western Civilization* (Leiden: Brill, 2011). The controversy between Niall Fergusson and Pankaj Mishra in the *London Review of Books*, November 3, 10, and 17, 2011, shows that the issue still has life in it.

28. Dipesh Chakrabarty, *Provincializing Europe: Postcolonial Thought and Historical Difference* (Princeton, NJ: Princeton University Press, 2007).

Hodgson and the New World History

CHAPTER FIVE

The Invention of World History from the Spirit of Nonviolent Resistance

Michael Geyer

Nonnulla enim pars inventionis est, nosse quid quaeras.[1]

Marshall Hodgson was not in the habit of quoting Augustine as many of his contemporaries did. But he would have endorsed Augustine's insistence that in catastrophic times any inquiry and especially historical inquiry depends on what kind of questions you ask. Marshall Hodgson wanted to know what it took to understand a world shaken by global war. His solution was to radically rethink world history and, as a means to that end, to teach and write an encompassing history of Islam and Islamicate societies. World history, while eschewing relativism, had to free itself from the "optical illusion" of a merely regional approach writ large.[2] To do world history right required instigating an epistemic revolution, and he thought that he might be the historian—it had to be a historian!—who could do so. The current essay explores the biographical sources for his conviction and the implication of his stance for teaching and writing world history.

Hodgson's scholarly career ended abruptly and prematurely in 1968 with much of his work unfinished.[3] Posthumous publications have changed the balance, but the asymmetry remains.[4] Hodgson's actual publications do not capture the extent of his work and the intellectual effort invested into it. While this is true for his Islamic history, it is most palpably the case for his writing on world history. The visible record of his publications, three unjustly forgotten scholarly essays, and the concluding conceptual and methodological sections of a draft manuscript titled "The Unity of World History: An Essay on Medieval and Modern Eurasia" provide a scant appreciation of the depth and the fiery thrust of Hodgson's work.[5] The latter only emerges from his invisible archive as it appears in the papers he left at his death.

This archive is a mere eight linear feet that once fit into a couple of fireproof filing cabinets.[6] It reveals a fearless, disconcertingly unconventional and piercing scribbler, who produced an abundance of often-scintillating snippets of notes, letters, and papers but struggled all his life to make himself understood—not least to himself—and to write (notwithstanding the three-volume *Venture of Islam*) coherently in long form.[7] Hodgson is a good case for "wild theorizing"—he even labeled one of his archival folders "wild historical theorizing"—a decade before Lévi-Strauss came up with his theory of the mind in its untamed state.[8] Augustine was among the wild historical theorizers, but it is Hodgson's mind in its untamed state that invented world history in the spirit of nonviolent resistance.

* * * *

In a lengthy letter to the anthropologist A. L. Kroeber, Hodgson explained that his interest in world history dated back to 1940 or 1941, when he was an undergraduate student at the University of Colorado.[9] By 1946 he had written a lengthy essay on world history.[10] Both the letter and the essay are missing. However, Hodgson's archive contains a syllabus, "Outlines of World History," which he sent off in summer 1942 to someone ("George") at the University of Colorado with an elaborate rationale for world history. In the early fifties he labeled this effort "first MGSH world history proposal."[11] In any case, Hodgson's initial foray into world history coincides with World War II and more specifically with the American entry into the war.

In the event that the course he had suggested was ever taught, Hodgson would have been unable to attend it, because he "had to leave in December 1942 and graduate under special war-time arrangements," as he put it in his 1959 curriculum vitae.[12] He moved from Colorado to Earlham College in Indiana, where he concentrated on "Relief and Reconstruction" in the hope of overseas deployment as a humanitarian aid worker. Instead, he was interned between 1943 and 1945 as part of the Civilian Public Service (CPS) in a conscientious-objector forestry camp, Camp Elkton, in Oregon.[13] After the war ended, he was released, but served another mandated year as orderly at the Concord State (psychiatric) Hospital in New Hampshire. The Oregon work camps were incubators of radical and "fervently religious" thought in the arts and the humanities.[14] Concord State Hospital, for its part, gave him the opportunity to write. For Hodgson his internment and CPS work were the catalyst for a new and revolutionary "outlook" in world history.

It is easy to underestimate what a huge leap it was—and always remained—for Hodgson to end up with history. When sharing his first world history texts in summer 1942, he left no doubt that he was "no historian."[15] Neither was he, as his concentration suggested, an economist. Rather more tellingly he occupied himself throughout his undergraduate years with what appears to have been an old high school project—to write a Life of Jesus.[16] This was not another historical Life. Rather, he started on the evangelical presupposition of an unmediated relation to Jesus, because Jesus was the "Light that lightens every man"[17]—an uncontroversial argument for a Quaker, but an impossible one for a budding (world) historian. For Hodgson, this gap between the unmediated presence of the past and its reflexive and critical rendition as history never fully closed. However, inasmuch as it was a source of tension in Hodgson's "intellectual experience,"[18] it was also a source of inspiration. Hodgson's turn to world history in 1940–42 would have not occurred had it not been for his Quaker faith in the unmediated access to the Light, which empowered him to see things stripped of their symbolic or rhetorical drapery.[19] Much later, in the 1960s, he would see and admire this quality in Sufi mystics.[20]

The world seen through the eyes of a Quaker was the source for his world-historical inspiration. At Colorado it all started with an ever-increasing involvement in campus affairs. He became a member of the (Methodist) Wesley Foundation, the Men's Essay Club, and the Fellowship of Reconciliation, and, in 1942, he joined the Cosmopolitan Club, which fought for desegregation—a cause that he would support for the rest of his life.[21] In the same year, he also quite suddenly began to write up a storm over pacifism and conscientious objection.[22] Hodgson's position with regard to both subjects was complex and evolving. He increasingly came to criticize mainstream Quakers, who in his view had chosen an accommodationist and quietist course of action, when he wanted to see heightened activism.[23] Merely abstaining from fighting was not enough. But his activism also separated him from isolationist pacifists. He was not out to draw America into splendid isolation, but set out to develop strategies and social action to mobilize for peace worldwide. As a pacifist he was a radical internationalist. He came out proudly and openly proclaiming his conscientious objection; he was ready to go underground in order to testify for his beliefs; he turned into a "militant" activist for peace. Thus, he embraced the CPS camps as a means of "setting up parallel social situations" with the purpose of creating societies of resisters.[24] He saw the camps as schools for collective, nonviolent action. "We must discipline ourselves in the techniques of nonviolence. . . . We must remake ourselves. . . . We must learn to be scorned."[25] As was the case with many civil rights activists,[26] Gandhi was Hodgson's hero and indeed his "saint."[27]

Hodgson threw himself into battle, literally, for a worldwide campaign for nonviolent resistance against war and oppression.[28] His antiwar, pacifist agenda was proactive, concerned with making peace and maintaining it. This entailed the realization that in a global war the struggle for peace had to be global as well. In his wildest dreams he imagined a worldwide, nonviolent, Satyagraha "police" force—local nonviolent mobilizations that used global support to achieve their end.[29] Nonviolent action was the proactive element of conscientious objection in war. Nonviolence separated him from the Marxists (real and imagined), because "opposition to war includes opposition to violent revolution."[30]

It also separated him from interwar isolationism of the nationalist or communitarian variety, because nonviolent struggle necessarily built on the recognition of an interconnected world. The latter, of course, was a common idea in the internationalist 1940s and had been building for quite some time, often with an anti-empire edge.[31] Hodgson was not one to fudge the issue. He held—right at the apex of global American war making—that the war demonstrated the end of European and, indeed, Western dominance and demonstrated "the general but varying resurgencies of the dominated lands."[32] It was one of Hodgson's cardinal intuitions that the struggle for self-assertion in the dominated world was the "historic" subtext of World War II—a struggle, both open and subterraneous, over the future of the world. All of them posed the choice between violence and nonviolence—in Japan, where it failed, and in India, where it might yet prevail. In order for these struggles to remain nonviolent, the "world outlook" in the dominant world needed to change in order for local nonviolent campaigns to succeed.

All this and more—there *is* more to it—came down to a simple proposition. Opposition to war was never to be passive. Mere conscientious objection was not enough. Rather, the latter had to develop quite literally into a force in its own right, because what was needed in order for peace to prevail was a revolution of consciousness—a "revolution in mental health fully comparable to the industrial revolution."[33] This revolution needed "spiritual grounding" as a prerequisite of unity and to that end it needed—world history! Why? World history, Hodgson argued in May 1942, was the way to advance "the possibility of overcoming the net of habit, social and personal, which overlays all our human relations and reactions." It was a means "not to be swept along in a blind rush of habituated and habituating events."[34] Stepping back into the past, into many pasts, world history opened the possibility to assess one's own "cultural situation" by relating it "in perspective to the rest of the world's history."[35]

History thus became a force of change. Over time, Hodgson went far beyond this and came to explore the potential of History as a prophetic force.[36] Kerygmatic history became Hodgson's lifelong obsession, but in the context of this essay this is just to suggest that there is yet more of an edge to Hodgson's discovery of world history than meets the eye.[37]

The purpose of world history, as conceived by Hodgson in 1942, was to set in motion an epistemic revolution—a "revolution in mental health" as Hodgson put it. It was the epistemological faculty of history as world history to engender this revolution. This was also what the world-historical situation required. In a breathtaking coda to an outline of world-historical development, he paused to reflect. The physical means for a resolution of the struggle for economic security were within reach. War had manifested a real-existing, interconnected "world community." Economies had sprawled, materially and physically, across the globe. And yet, the spirit—"the light," or the (self-)consciousness of human beings living in an interconnected world—was missing. The world's religions, all of them, which had been expanding beyond regions and empires over more than a thousand years, had begun, in the face of this new condition, "to monumentally reverse themselves in an orgy of selfishness." They had come to shrink from the challenge of the modern world, which was to be in their respective ways the light of an actually existing, physical and material, world community. A resolution of the spiritual unity of the world, building on the diverse religious traditions, was nowhere in sight.[38] Worldwide material connections had created an infrastructure, but would and could not in and of themselves generate on a world scale what religions had achieved on a regional and transregional level over the past two thousand years—to create an awareness, a consciousness of the unity of the world in all its diversity.

In February 1949, by now a graduate student at the University of Chicago focusing on Islamic history with Gustave von Grunebaum, he delivered on the 1942 promise with a first syllabus "Toward a Course in World History." Its purpose was "to give background to world community / to express the variety, wonder and tragedy of life / to give perspective against particular historical assumptions / to give historical foundation for an open approach to problems against the dead ends of various cultural systems."[39] Lest there be any doubt, Western civilization shared in this predicament.

* * * *

Most scholars come to world history under the influence of other scholars. Reading world history begets world historians.[40] By contrast, Hodgson was thrown into world history in a Pauline mode.[41] He was shaken to the core by the US entry into World War II, which he instantly read as a "global war." World history in the spirit of nonviolent resistance was his response to the epiphany, and the radical critique of the Western distortion of "world outlook," fully articulated by 1945–46, was its main outcome.

During his CPS years he became a voracious reader and thanks to his invisible archive of notes we can reconstruct for the most part how he built the case for a new world history. This was always a tentative and open-ended process. For one, Hodgson was not at all sure whether history could provide a sufficient answer to the challenge. He thought that world history might rather be the subject for "epic poetry"—an idea that he pursued throughout his life, but wisely kept hidden from his more academic-minded colleagues.[42] Discerning historians will find traces of this fascination in his *Venture*. For another, he did not think very highly of preceding historians of world civilizations, Arnold Toynbee among them, though he read them all.[43] Instead, he rummaged widely in anthropology and philosophy of history. A. L. Kroeber among anthropologists and G. W. F. Hegel among philosophers (and Karl Marx in the Hegelian slipstream) proved crucial early on. But it is telling that Giambattista Vico among the Western classics and the neo-Kantian Heinrich Rickert among the moderns also figured prominently. They indicate a turn toward a critical historical hermeneutics, which Hodgson labored over all his life in an effort to find ways to acknowledge irreducible difference in world civilizations while maintaining their common humanity.[44] From the very start, however, he also read widely and deeply into non-Western literatures and histories, including those of East Asia. While Mahatma Gandhi and the much-praised Jawaharlal Nehru might be considered "Westernized," the same could not be said of the historian, legal scholar, and exegete of the Quran Muhammad ibn Jarir al-Tabari (AD 838–923), whose name appears in a record of an exploratory visit to the University of Chicago Library in 1943.[45] Hodgson's readings befitted his iconoclastic mind and his radical project to construct a new world history.

A first essay in a Quaker journal for social-studies teachers in 1944 and a heretofore overlooked short piece in the *Friends' Intelligencer* give an indication where all this might lead.[46] The 1944 and 1946 essays tried to convey the message that the current war called for a dramatic change in perception. A transformative kind of history—world history—was needed in order to abandon the prevalent Eurocentric outlook. This outlook did not reflect the demographic realities of the world nor did it get the civilizational contribution of world civilizations right. It foreshortened the world's pasts, delivering a "distorted picture of the world."[47] "To 'think globally' is to think in terms of the whole globe, rather than in terms of our conventional provincialism."[48] Religions of the Mosaic tradition, Christians and Muslims in particular, must avoid "religious imperialism" and "bigotry," which cannot but lead to violence.

Hodgson delivered these chastisements with carefully reasoned and "evidenced" arguments and had practical suggestions to offer to social-studies teachers on how to avoid the traps of "provincialism" and "distortion."[49] World history properly done would not just be the more truthful history, but its real value was "in breaking down our [American] ethnocentrism," because America's position in the world was "strong, to be sure, but precarious" and would come to depend ever more on the non-Western world.[50] Hodgson's suggestions for scholarship were tentative, but a program and a project were set—"to study the history of the world as a whole, and not in the unbalanced way we have pretended to study it." In so doing, "we would discover that European history . . . has in the main, at least until recently, been a *dependent* part of the general development of the world."[51] The catchphrase for all this was the "westward distortion in history."[52]

For Christians, this meant that a "truly universal Church" did not think of the world as a "field of mission in need of our control," but as "fellow churches" everywhere. "Global religion" discovered "the spirit"—elsewhere Hodgson spoke of "the light"—that united them in their inalienable difference.[53]

For social-studies teachers Hodgson stressed three points. America had to overcome its provincialism; Europe had to be decentered; and Asia had to be de-orientalized. Hodgson publicized these points in a combination of patient, didactic exposition and willful epistemic assertion. He offered some simple tools to achieve his goal. The Mercator projection for world maps needed to be abandoned, because its distortions were wrong and useless. If Europe is to be made into a "continent," do the same for India, but better use the term Eurasia and then subdivide the hemisphere into many regions. Asia is not a continent, but many civilizations; respect them and don't divide the East (Asia) and the West (Europe/US) into two complementary halves of world civilization. In a 1945 book project Hodgson used this provocative exclamation: "THERE IS NO ORIENT."[54]

In 1945–46 Hodgson busied himself with hunting down "distortions in World History" and produced quite a delicious rogues' gallery of "horrible examples."[55] He collected material for an article on "actions historians should take with regard to the little details that distort historical and geographical perspective" and proved to be a lifelong pest when it came to "terminology."[56]

Then again, more clearly and more radically than his teachers and, later on, colleagues at the University of Chicago, he recognized that changing the American "world outlook" was an all-encompassing task, because distortions of the world picture were "habitual," deeply ingrained in the way Americans (and Europeans) experienced the world. In short, they were epistemic.

By far his most consequential observations concerned history. It was wrong, he argued, to put European culture "in the center of the stage of world history."[57] Europe was far more isolated than India from world-historical developments for most of recorded history. One of the consequences of this argument—explicit already in 1944,[58] and subsequently one of the main bones of contention with William McNeill and, more generally, with the Braudel school of Mediterranean-world history[59]—was his shift from a Rome-centric to a Byzantine/Persian/Indian Ocean–centric world picture.[60] It was doubly wrong to think of non-Western cultures as dead. They might have been overwhelmed, but the " 'slow march westward of civilization' [is] a fiction . . . useful to some American nationalists."[61]

This take on Western provincialism had consequences. Because of the pervasive, experiential nature of the Western "world outlook," conventional scholarly specializations would not suffice to overcome it. One of the first of Hodgson's many book projects, "Outline of a book combatting Western provincialism," also called "Western Provincialism—its falsities & symptoms,"[62] makes clear that the project of remaking a global worldview would by necessity have to be interdisciplinary and involve all the humanities and social sciences as well as religious life. In 1952, Hodgson, in one of his obsessive moods, scribbled down what it would take to launch a campaign against the Mercator projection.[63] It involved historians to develop an inventory of the uses of Mercator; geographers to explore the uses of world projections; psychologists to study perception and attitudes; and "public-relations men" to analyze how the projection was sold. Doing world history needed both interdisciplinary scholarship and a distinctly practice-oriented, public-policy dimension. It literally meant to be "campaigning."

Still at Camp Elkton, in 1945, Hodgson had penned an outline, which marks the transition from youthful protest to a program of study. The brief text has the rather unpromising title "Handbook of World Citizenship."[64] The title of the project seems to suggest a peroration along the lines of Maynard Hutchins, president of the University of Chicago and well-known "one-worlder," or of Quincy Wright, eminent social-science professor at the same university.[65] But already then, Hodgson was capable of surprise. He did identify the purpose of the prospective book in the fashion of the time. It was to serve "humanity as a community." However, a world historian would have to explore not only the territorial order of the world, but also what we nowadays might call the phantom borders and frontiers of the world—the divisions by religion and language and the inequalities of race in particular that cut across territories. Later on, he would argue that there was another world, as it were, underlying the world of states, and this was a world of social and cultural complexes or "life-orientations." When in February 1968, mere months before his death, Hodgson put together a list of projects, he listed the "World Citizen Handbook" among other urgent world history projects, because he argued that transborder "life-orientations" were shaping the future of the world.[66]

In 1945 though, he rather picked up the theme of "combatting . . . provincialism." World community is served, he argued, by overcoming "*our* ignorance & misinformation; *our* nationalism & ethnocentrism." Its purpose was not to salvage others and to impose world community on them, but to reorient who *we* are as citizens. To this end, Hodgson surmised it was essential to acknowledge the main challenges of the present world—"political (war); economic and financial (trade—depression); social (migration—minorities)." All this required the recognition that "we" as citizens of the United States were part of the world and, although immensely powerful, not capable of shaping its future peacefully without radical reorientation. Such small differences of subject-position in relation to the one-worlders had large consequences.

Among the main academic problems in pursuing this kind of self-consciously global history project he listed "problems of cooperative scholarship" and the use of "symbolic logic" (as a unifying "language" of analysis) as top priorities for study.[67] Traditional, individualistic modes of scholarship were ineffective in view of the richness of world history, but more cooperative scholarship needed a language of cooperation—not least in light of the difference of world-historical traditions. None of the envisioned cooperative work was realized in Hodgson's lifetime. A grant application that would have allowed Hodgson (together with Herman Sinaiko) to pursue his orientalism project on a minor scale failed.[68] It is indicative that only the editors of the UNESCO Courier in Paris got excited and repeatedly printed versions of Hodgson's antiorientalist essays. However, even there Hodgson's starkest manifesto against Mercator and in favor of a reorientation of the geographic imagination was published only posthumously.[69]

Hodgson's campaign, aside from being stuck in his invisible archive, had none of the literary flourish of Edward Said's intervention some thirty years later, though it had the same urgency.[70] His youthful enthusiasm for Gandhi-style nonviolent action in 1942 took shape in the form of a history, by necessity a world-encompassing history, whose purpose it was to generate an epistemic revolution. Replacing the Mercator projection, revamping terminology and chronology, remapping the world and its history—all of this served the purpose of seeing the "global world" anew and to that end to alter sense perception. "The problem of reorienting ourselves to a more interregional viewpoint," he argued, "is psychologically far-reaching and must be solved along with that of organizing the historical material."[71] This reorientation would require changing the "experience" of orienting oneself in the world. For Hodgson this ultimately was a spiritual challenge.

As Europe was decentered and the United States deprovincialized, world history would have to overcome its habitual "westward distortion" and its "world outlook" would have to be cosmopolitanized.[72] The challenge consisted in shrinking Europe to its proper size while introducing the world in its true historical proportions—and to develop a critical comparative method to accomplish that end.[73] The challenge was to recognize the unity of the world as well as the inalienable difference of its cultures and religions. Hodgson set out not so much to interpret the world as to change it—that is to change the world picture, within which people understand and experience the world. This was the task of world history.

* * * *

Hodgson developed his initial insight about the "westward distortion of history" and its associated critique of orientalism into a world history project that fellow historians had difficulty comprehending at the time. He set out to develop an *inter*regional and *inter*civilizational history of the world and did so by envisioning an Afro-Eurasian hemisphere as a connected commons. Of course, world historians before him had always known, and to varying degrees emphasized, relationships between civilizations. However, for Hodgson connectivity was the pivot from which to reorder and to reorganize the area of world history. He faced similar problems with his Islamic history, which he conceived as a history of Islamicate societies rather than of a rooted Islam.[74] Contemporary historians have a somewhat different problem of comprehension. While Hodgson emphasized and, indeed, prioritized connectivity, he was not interested in mobility as such, but in the question of where and in which way mobile cultures and religions as well as people(s) and things settled over time. Both together make up world history.

Hodgson had developed the idea of world history as an interconnected history already in 1945–46, adapting A. L. Kroeber's concept of an "oikoumene."[75] But it was only in 1954 that he published a much shorter piece, "Hemispheric Inter-regional History as an Approach to World History." The immediate cause for picking up the 1946 essay after the completion of his thesis in Islamic history and after postdoctoral years at Aligarh Muslim University in India and at the University of Frankfurt in Germany was his deep dissatisfaction with the UNESCO-sponsored Scientific and Cultural History of Mankind.[76] One of the editors of that history, the Chicago history professor Louis R. Gottschalk, confirmed his worst expectations about Western provincialism. When challenged that his volume in the UNESCO series omitted the role of Islam in world history, Gottschalk replied that due to the lack of sources the history of Islam could not be written—and if it were written nevertheless, nobody would be interested in reading it.[77] The more remote cause was Hodgson's postdoctoral employment in the Ford Foundation's Comparison of Cultures Program at the University of Chicago that was run by Robert Redfield and Milton Singer. While they were supportive of Hodgson's world history endeavors, Hodgson feared that they never quite understood his project.[78] Hodgson was not happy with just filling the Islamic niche in comparative world civilizations, even if Islamic civilization received equal treatment, nor did he approve of Redfield and Singer's notion of civilization. While he agreed with them on the centrality of "culture" (insisting that religion was a key element), he rejected the essentialist and closed nature of their understanding of civilizations and protested against their atemporal and anachronistic comparisons.[79]

Hodgson's revised 1946 manuscript was rejected by *South Atlantic Quarterly*, but it got none less than Lucien Febvre excited. Guy Métraux, secretary general of the International Commission for a Scientific and Cultural History of Mankind, related the news. François Crouzet, no minor historian in his own right, relayed that the master "much appreciated" Hodgson's paper, which was promptly accepted by the editorial board in January.[80] It appeared in the first volume of the *Cahiers d'histoire mondiale*. Hodgson was somewhat surprised by the lack of opposition in Paris, because Gottschalk had fired him up for setting the commission right on their misbegotten UNESCO world history project. "MUST PERSUADE these people of the need for perspective."[81] In the event, *The Foundations of the Modern World* did not change much.[82] But Hodgson wrote a second essay for the *Cahiers*, "The Unity of Later Islamic History," which was crucial for conceptualizing both his Islamic and his world history.[83]

His ambitions had become quite academic by 1954. Hodgson suggested in his essay a way of thinking "the world" as a researchable entity—focusing on the Eurasian-African or eastern "hemisphere"—rather than envisioning it as a galaxy of civilizations that was lined up in some overall logic of human development. It is telling that Edward D'Arms from the Rockefeller Foundation saw the main advantage of Hodgson's idea in its practicability.[84] The intellectually more challenging point was that a hemispheric history broke with world history as a deep history of Europe, because as hemispheric history it had no single pivot in space. It accommodated a multiplicity of actors at any one time and shifting pivots of world-historical development over time. It raised the question of comparative development, but did so by historicizing the relative position of societies and entire civilizations in time in the context of interregional historical development.

The single most important aspect of the essay was to think of the area of world history as a spatially interconnected (Afro-Eurasian) hemisphere.[85] Hodgson knew perfectly well that the Americas constituted another hemispheric area of world history, but in prioritizing connectivity over parallel or comparative human development he excluded the Americas from his considerations up to the point when the two hemispheric histories reconverged. He would revisit his position time and again, trying to accommodate a more open-ended human history, but his emphasis on hemispheric inter*relational* history undercut these efforts. Yet it should also be said that even for the postconquest era he never came to grips with the hemisphere in which he was writing. His world history was a Eurasian and by extension Eurasian-African history.

Hodgson's main contention is that Eurasia-Africa is best understood as a single zone of exchange of literate urban civilizations. Exchange would ultimately transport any kind of innovation (mechanical, spiritual, social, or economic) across the entire space. Regional civilizational clusters were connected in a contiguous history of cohabitation, which is why regional/civilizational developments were inseparable from the overall development of the entire zone. The "hemisphere" was in actual fact a zone of cohabitation. "The major Eurasian civilizations can be considered as regions within a single historical configuration. Seen from this angle, the societies studied in the civilizational courses and by the specialists in the various areas tend to lose their independent, self-contained characters and become, rather, interrelated and interdependent part of a single, inclusive region [Eurasian-African zone] with an overall pattern of historical development."[86] This approach suggests an open-ended spatial and interactive history, and in many ways this is the attraction of Hodgson's approach that everyone recognized at the time. Hodgson called this dimension of world history the "interregional historical constellation." This constellation consisted of several regional clusters, which reproduced themselves as separate entities while continuously adjusting to the overall constellation.

Connectivity was the constituting and constitutive feature of the Afro-Eurasian ecumene. Hence the genuine subject of interregional history as world history was not the succession of civilizations or of societies and empires within civilizations, but the regime of conscious and unconscious influences that connected them. Civilizational influences spread out, expanding "civilized territory,"[87] but more crucially no part of this Eurasian world ever developed in isolation. World-historical development was the opposite of a succession of civilizational monads. This meant first and foremost exchange within the privileged band of citied civilizations, but Hodgson was not prejudiced. When he argued that "the remainder [the nonliterate, nonurban part of the world] must recognize the dominance of the [Eurasian] cultural heritage,"[88] he was thinking of the far west of Europe and of Southeast Asia as much as of Central Asia and the far south (sub-Saharan Africa).

For much of world history the far west was at the margins of the Eurasian ecumene, which was crucially shaped by the Middle East, South Asia, and the Far East. He noted the relative isolation of—or rather the distance to—East Asia in relation to the rest of Eurasia, but emphasized the key role of China as a motor of innovation. East Asia (China) developed in relative isolation, but was never at the margin of the Eurasian constellation, which the European peninsula most definitely was.[89]

As might be expected, much of Hodgson's world history project was dedicated to correcting Western distortions of the spatial and temporal unfolding of world history. In this context, the history of an expansive Islam figured most prominently, because it had reached farther and deeper than any other civilization until the most recent era. This was in many ways the subtext of *Venture*, but it was also the subject of the essay(s) "Islam in World History."[90] Hodgson highlighted what Shahab Ahmed recently called the "Balkans-to-Bengal complex."[91] What Ahmed treats as the axis of "mature Islam" and, hence, as an intra-Islamic phenomenon, Hodgson used in its earliest instantiation to resituate the interregional history of the Eurasian-African hemisphere. This complex meeting and mixing point of civilizations emerged as the pivotal subregion of world history.[92] If Braudel and, in his wake, William McNeill pivoted their histories on a restless Mediterranean—Braudel with an emphasis on the western and McNeill with an emphasis on the eastern Mediterranean—Hodgson resolutely rejected this "view" as a Western distortion in favor of the enduring import of the fertile crescent, stretching from the Mediterranean to the Indian Ocean littoral, as the crossroad of an interconnected Eurasian hemisphere. In this context it must remain an unresolved puzzle why Hodgson's papers are silent about this classic geopolitical layout of world history, and we can only speculate at this point that Hodgson came to it by way of Islamic rather than by way of European history.[93]

While much of the excitement of the 1954 essay concerned the spatial layout of the interconnected hemisphere, the crux of the essay is its treatment of time and of historicity. The complications have to do with the history of connectivity and how to approach it. The essay underscored the significance of connectivity, but not quite the way we might imagine. In misappropriating Kroeber's term "oikoumene," which Hodgson subsequently replaced with what he called with some variations "an interregional historical complex," he set up an argument that he never fully unraveled. He rejected quite intuitively the "flat earth" idea of (ever-denser) interactions despite his emphasis on connectivity. He rather stuck to the notion of an "ecumene" as a common home (with more central and more marginal spaces for interaction) and he was interested in the changing interior and exterior architecture of this common home.

In the first instance, he privileged the history of urban societies and their aggregation, civilizational clusters that stretched across the entire Eurasian-African land mass. Mobile societies did figure prominently as disruptors as well as transmitters—so much so that he earned the wrath of some of his colleagues in Islamic history for (over)emphasizing merchants and pilgrims over imperial bureaucrats and generals.[94] But his focus was on settled urban societies as "cosmopolitan" actors, as we would say today. That is, he was interested in urban societies in their interconnectivity.

So far, so good. Of course, Toynbee had claimed this much for his civilizations, but he did not think of this connectivity as the very core of world history. Hodgson made a daring leap in the opposite direction, but this leap had less to do with the fact of connectivity than with "placing" connectivity in space. Each of the clusters of urban societies, he argued, had its dense microhistories, but world history proper proceeded on a stage too wide for any one local or regional history to define an entire hemisphere. "From a world-historical point of view what is important is not European [or any regional] history in itself, however important that be for us all; but its role in interregional history."[95] World history was thus not the sum total of all civilizational histories, but it was the surfeit that exceeded any one regional history and yet connected them all—and more, that changed and shaped all of them in real time.

Hodgson struggled mightily to explain what this "extra" consisted of and why it should not be confused with the "meta" of philosophical history. He insisted that "the whole," the hemisphere, was always larger than its parts. In its simplest form, this meant to say that the history of any one part always implicated the entire hemisphere. A more complex formulation of the same observation suggested that world history could not be the mere accumulation of separate histories, but had to focus on the developments they had in common. While the commonality of development could be discussed in terms of (disconnected) parallel developments (Kroeber, Redfield) or in terms of diffusion from a center (Toynbee, McNeill), Hodgson favored what he referred to as a "contextual" approach.[96] In his 1954 essay this contextual approach was barely visible, and yet it was the innovation on which the entire essay as well as his world history depended.

If connectivity mattered, connectivity in its aggregate state mattered more: Hodgson argued that in the sum total of interactions (themselves varying over time) some interaction-"events" proved to be pivotal, while others were not—and these pivotal, "extra-ordinary" "events" made a difference. This was easiest to explain with reference to violent disruptions such as the rise of Mongol power, but Hodgson put more emphasis on the transformative impact of the soft power of religion and knowledge. Hodgson stressed the act of creative disruption—be it the formation of Islam, the shaping of an ascetic-monastic ideal (in South Asia) or the industrial revolution (and its scientific mindset). Within a connected world he put a premium on these civilization-altering innovations, which, he argued, shaped "*the general disposition of the Hemisphere*."[97]

The dynamic of hemispheric and intercivilizational developments up to and in the wake of disposition-setting events was the proper subject of world history. The crucial argument here is that the pattern of overall development was *not* guided by one or the other meta-logic—neither Hegel's development toward freedom nor capitalism as a world system. Rather it was initiated by discrete macro-"events" of civilizational innovation and transformation. If connectivity was the normal state of the world, these transformative events reshaped the disposition of the entire hemisphere. "World history must be seen not only as network of various contacts and cultural diffusions among several nations and civilizations. It displays a common context of continuously changing conditions which affect both the interrelations among societies and the possibilities of their internal development."[98] It is as if a new wing were added to the edifice or a new conversation introduced—and every other cluster of societies took notice, was shocked out of its comfort, emulated the innovation and adjusted to it within its own capacity. For most of history or, in any case, Hodgson's world history, the always painful capacity for emulation assured that civilizations retained their differences while incorporating new thoughts, new technologies, and new beliefs. This is why the expansion of Islam amounted to the spreading of plural Islamicate societies. Hodgson's world history was in essence a history of civilization-level disruption and innovation in the Eurasian-African hemisphere.

That urban, literate societies learned and borrowed from each other, that imperial conquests impressed life orientations on entire populations, and that conversions typically ran ahead of empire (and that the success of Islam in its time had more to do with conversion than with domination)—all these are contestable claims, empirical variations of a basic proposition, which comes in three parts.[99] The first one is that there was never one-world, but always many, though not an infinite number of worlds. More difficult to countenance is the second and conjoined argument: these worlds developed separately, but they were part of a single habitat of literate, citied societies—an "ecumenic configuration." Third, both particular cultures and civilizational clusters as well as the configuration at large metamorphosed or transmuted over time. These changes, we might deduce, amounted to epistemic "transmutations."

While the insistence on the historicity of hemispheric development—"the general disposition of the Hemisphere"—made sense in the abstract, the concept was immensely difficult to translate into actual history. It was well and good to think of hemispheric development as a historical construct rather than a metahistorical (natural, metaphysical, or historiographical) contrivance. But while Hodgson recognized the importance of scale in world history, he had trouble identifying what exactly pertained to world history and what did not. He never fully settled the issue. Rather, in his world history writing he did exactly what he had advised against in his 1954 essay—settling with a less-than-world-historical scale that incorporated separate and interactive histories across the hemisphere. In theory he rather favored epistemic "configurations" or "historical dispositions" that extended over a very long time and accommodated a host of discrete histories. In practice, he eventually ended somewhere in between in his (unfinished) draft of a world history, which lagged behind his theorizing, but for that had the advantage of being eminently readable.[100]

* * * *

These, then, are the key contentions that shaped Hodgson's world history: "The world" is more than the sum of its civilizations; it is an interconnected ecumene, configuration, or constellation. The nature of this interconnectedness as well as the pivots of interconnection have changed over time; interconnectedness has its own historicity. The history of humanity was not "flat." Civilizational clusters were in permanent flux—because they interacted with each other, but ultimately because human creativity (meaning making, world making) sooner rather than later set new bars for everyone. We might interpolate that this is why a marginal far west (Europe) could get a leg up and this is why Hodgson was confident that India, China, and one part or another of the Islamicate world would resurface after the Western onslaught. This latter point was made loud and clear already in 1962, albeit in a Pakistani journal.[101] And as a reprise of where Hodgson started out, he insisted that none of these transformations could be understood, that world history would necessarily fail coming to grips with the past and the present, if world historians persisted in holding on to the Western distortion of the "world outlook."

Hodgson's 1954 intervention raised a host of problems, which he struggled to resolve with mixed success in the ensuing years. His 1963 essay "The Inter-relations of Societies in History" clarifies some of the contentions in his earlier essay(s) and provides a narrative outline for a potential book. But as published essays are wont to do, it smoothed out the rough edges, the disputations, and above all the turmoil of thinking that make Hodgson's archive so fascinating. Three of these tempests are of particular interest—the nature of historical progress, the condition of the present, and the place of history as a force for changing the world.

First, the question of progress in history arose early on, in the mid-forties, in Hodgson's debates with Marxism. He once again picked up the concern when he turned to the issue of Arabic and especially Turkish and Egyptian modernization, which occupied him far more than the published record would suggest.[102] In his mind, the question of progress was inseparable from the much-debated issue of diffusion, which he rejected, as we have seen.

Hodgson pushed this argument a decisive step further, when he introduced Husserl's term "life-orientation," roughly equivalent to the present notion of world making and meaning making.[103] No "life-orientation," he argued, ever had a complete answer to spiritual and material meaning and world making, be it on a grand cosmic or an everyday-life scale. Inasmuch as any given society within a civilizational complex found a moment of stability, it would either decay or be undercut for any number of reasons, including of course lateral pressures in an interconnected world. It was wrong, therefore, to think of any society as complete in itself, even if there were precious moments in each civilization of dazzling achievement, when harmonious societies seemed to rest in themselves. Such moments of brilliance were fleeting, even if their world-historical impact extended through time and space. Tension and contradiction were the norm. The "genius" (A. L. Kroeber) of life orientations consisted in the creative energy of individuals, entire societies, and civilizational clusters engendering, or borrowing, solutions in a permanently unstable or fallible world.[104] While "solutions"—technical or scientific interventions, as much as spiritual practices such as asceticism and mysticism—traveled, they did not dissipate, but were appropriated and reinvented in place after place and fitted in.[105] For Hodgson this explained why knowledge and techniques traveled and, yet, civilizational differences persisted. Hence, Islam differentiated into Islamicate societies and the transmission of legacies (like Aristotle's philosophy or Indian mathematics) was a robust process of (re)invention and innovation.

Historical development rather than being a continuous process, whether linear or cyclical, becomes a matter of choice and invention—and of lateral competition and conflict over choices, once they were taken. Hodgson thus saved an important place for contingency in world history. "I see historical events as the resolution of one disequilibrium into a new disequilibrium calling for a new resolution. Correspondingly, I conceive of society and a culture in the form of a cultural tradition of interchange and dialog among a given group, grounded in that group's commitment to initial creative moments (economic, intellectual, even spiritual), and in its response to the continuing consequences: both to the internal unfolding of the implications of those commitments, and to the evolving external environment imposing new group interests."[106] In one of his more delirious texts Hodgson notes "that in all systems, not only of history but of thought, we must begin with the assumption of inconsistency and inherent instability, the resolution of which is in turn unstable."[107] Contingency is the motor of development in world history!

A second concern caught up with Hodgson when he was faced with the precipitous rise of the West to world dominance. It was one thing to argue that this rise had not been foreordained since the beginning of time; that historically it had led to grievous distortions; that the age of European hegemony had been short, and so on. The only interesting aspect of this story is that almost any argument that has been made in the recent world-historical revival is already present in Hodgson's archive. However, none of his critiques solved the problem of how to assess the world-historical role of the West, once it occurred. What exactly was it that was rising? A decentered world history did not lack comparisons, but were they valid? Could the rise of the West be compared with the Mongol expansion or, perhaps, the dramatic rise of Islam? Was it at all comparable with the spread of Chinese civilization? Was "the West" a belief system and, if so, how did it differ from axial-age religions? Hodgson's answer remained tentative and inconclusive, but was no less bold for that. It came in two parts. The first one had to do with the difference between the world-historical role of Islam and the West, which he approached in a much revised and contested essay on Islam and Christianity.[108] Pivotal as Islamicate societies were in shaping the "general disposition of the [Afro-Eurasian] hemisphere," the power of Islam over the entire sphere was limited. Islam shaped the *disposition* of the entire ecumene perhaps more than any other civilization, but it did not overpower the world. By contrast the world-historical role of its European far west drastically reconfigured the architecture of the ecumenic "configuration." It was the equivalent of a genetic "transmutation."[109] It gave the configuration a material gestalt and physical presence, which he called "global constellation."[110] Hodgson was certain that this constellation no longer was "home." But he now also wondered: "Is the [technical transmutation] so much more massive that the place of man in nature must be rethought?"[111]

It took a former University of Chicago undergraduate from Indiana to remind Hodgson of what he was saying:[112] "I gather that in a great cultural complex, like that of Afro-Eurasia, we must expect that different elements will lead the procession at different times. . . . And it so happened that Europe was in the lead at a very critical time. This was the point where, for the first time, cultural superiority could be *carried* and *exploited* faster than it could be *transmitted* and *adapted*."[113] The European difference, in short, had a distinctly temporal dimension. In part, societies in the far west of the Eurasian ecumene remade themselves in a process of rapid acceleration. More important, for a moment in history, the velocity of this acceleration overwhelmed the time it took for societies to adapt. Once transmission and adaptation accelerated, the temporal advantage of Western superiority was undone. For Hodgson, this moment of reorientation had come in World War II, which, as we have seen, was the reason for the necessity of a new world outlook in the first place.

Hodgson worked out none of the implications of the Western "transmutation," but the basic argument is worth our attention. Hodgson argued in essence that "the great divergence" between the Western world and Eurasian civilizations could not be explained genealogically, even though the West had taken on the role of world-historical incubator that others had taken on before. The

Western difference consisted rather in the ability to control "global" connectivity for a brief historical moment, which necessarily had to vanish. In a rising Western world—as opposed to the preceding Islamic and the concurrent Chinese worlds—connectivity outraced the time necessary for self-transformation. Hodgson thought that this moment had ended with the rise of oppressed people since World War II. He would not at all have been astounded by the post-1970s transformation of the world. Connectivity is power; it is, if not the source, the reality of the "great divergence."[114]

The wider consequence of the rise of the far west was that the concepts of "ecumenic configuration" and "global constellation" articulated two radically different modes of "world order."[115] In contrast to ecumenic times, the "general disposition" of the "global constellation" entailed that emulation, adaptation, creative disruption, and cultural innovation occurred *within* a unified world. In 1952, just after having finished his year at Aligarh Muslim University, he concluded: "Mankind for the first time is ready for a global civilization—and ready to appreciate effectively all past civilizations."[116] Globality, in short, was the necessary condition for a unified world, which was becoming, Hodgson insisted, a post-occidental world, in which civilizational difference could and would be articulated. He left no doubt that this was a moment of epistemic rupture.

Third then, what was history to do in this situation? Hodgson was unequivocal, and his history of nonviolent resistance came full circle. It was imperative for historians to shake off the "western distortion of world history" and use the global condition to recognize all the worlds pasts. The first act of resistance in a global age was world *history*—the recovery of the world's traditions![117] A second act would have to be rethinking "man's place in nature," but while he began to read up on the scientific literature on the subject, admired Rachel Carson and demolished Teilhard de Chardin, he was just barely beginning to formulate a position.

An unpublished text on the requirements of world history, written in 1955, summarized these positions early on.[118] This text was less concerned with the how than with the why of world history. We are living, Hodgson argued, "in an age when a true world history becomes possible at least in scope," and it turns out that "we know little of the circumstances in which men have acted historically—biological, climatic, genetic, technological, geographical, intellectual, psychological, imaginative, political." But we do know what the challenge and the purpose of world history is. It is, first, "the purpose of all scholarship . . . to widen the human vision." It is, second, "to provide an orientation for all the great historical episodes, giving each a place in the whole [the pre-ecumenical, the ecumenic, and the global respectively] . . . replacing . . . misapprehensions and distortions . . . and leave the reader with nothing less than a fully human standpoint . . . bringing home the significance of the historical dimension of life." The critical task in all of this was to rediscover in the imbrication of global and local scales "the historical dimension of life," because without their past civilizations have lost their "moral heritage" and their integrity.[119] Writing world history therefore was an act of conscientious objection in an age that stripped civilizations of their past and history of its poetic and revelatory power. It was an act of resistance against narrow-minded ethnocentrism as much as against greedy cosmopolitanism.[120] Whether or not this history had to be a religious history or, in any case, a history of religion as Hodgson concluded is another matter.[121] What mattered is that the recovery of the many pasts of humankind was the creative disruption necessary to prepare the future—in all parts of the world.

Notes

1. Saint Augustine, *Questionum in Heptateuchum Libri Septem, Liber Primus: Quaestiones in Genesim, Prooemium, S. Aurelii Augustini Opera Omnia*, vol. 34; http://www.augustinus.it/latino/questioni_ettateuco/index2.htm, accessed August 5, 2017.

2. Marshall Hodgson's application for a Guggenheim fellowship, March 15, 1968; courtesy of the John Simon Guggenheim Memorial Foundation.

3. "Statement of my publications as foreseen as of now (excluding articles, of which I have published a great many and have several more in the hopper not quite ready yet to publish)," February 16, 1968, University of Chicago, Committee on Social Thought, Records, box 5, folder 6, Special Collections Research Center, University of Chicago Library (hereafter cited as CST).

4. Preeminently: Marshall G. S. Hodgson, *The Venture of Islam: Conscience and History in a World Civilization*, 3 vols. (Chicago: University of Chicago Press, 1974).

5. The entire manuscript is in the Marshall G. S. Hodgson Papers, box 14, folder 14, box 15, folders 1–6, and box 16, folder 1, Special Collections Research Center, University of Chicago Library (hereafter cited as Hodgson Papers). The selection is in *Rethinking World History: Essays on Europe, Islam, and World History*, ed. Edmund Burke III (Cambridge: Cambridge University Press, 1993), chaps. 11–13. The essays are "World History and a World Outlook," *Social Studies* (Washington, DC) 35 (1944): 297–301; "Hemispheric Inter-regional History as an Approach to World History," *Cahiers d'histoire mondiale* 1 (1954): 715–23; and "The Inter-relations of Societies in History," *Comparative Studies in Society and History* 5, no. 2 (1963): 227–50.

6. Phyllis Hodgson to Mrs. Armour [administrative secretary of the Committee on Social Thought], June 25, 1971, asking if the university can provide room for "Marshall's fireproof filing cabinets with all his writings in it"; CST, box 5, folder 4.

7. Hodgson to "Tom" Fallers, June 25, 1966, Lloyd A. Fallers Papers, box 7, folder 9, Special Collections Research Center, University of Chicago Library.

8. See Hodgson Papers, box 6, folder 12; Claude Lévi-Strauss, *La pensée sauvage* (Paris: Plon, 1962).

9. Hodgson to A. L. Kroeber, May 21, 1954, Hodgson Papers, box 15, folder 8.

10. See his Guggenheim application, p. 1. References to the "1946 essay" in Hodgson Papers, box 6, folder 23.

11. Hodgson to "George," with appendixes, June 6, 1942, with note in telltale green ink and Hodgson's hand, Hodgson Papers, box 6, folder 21. There was no "George" on the history faculty at the time, and no world history course was offered, though "staff" taught History 102, Historical Background of Current Problems. Email from David M. Hays, University Libraries, University of Colorado Boulder, January 24, 2017.

12. "Marshall Goodwin Simms Hodgson," January 20, 1959, CST, box 5, folder 4.

13. "CPS Unit Number 059-01: The Civilian Public Service Story," http://civilianpublicservice.org/camps/59/1, accessed December 10, 2016.

14. Steve McQuiddy, *Here on the Edge: How a Small Group of World War II Conscientious Objectors Took Art and Peace from the Margins to the Mainstream* (Corvallis: Oregon State University Press, 2013), 2. The quote is taken from fellow internee and poet William Everson. Hodgson speaks of "Socialist and pacifist-type activities" in an undated fragment, Hodgson Papers, box 15, folder 6.

15. Hodgson to "George," June 6, 1942, Hodgson Papers, box 6, folder 21.

16. Materials and drafts are in Hodgson Papers, box 5, folder 12.

17. "Quaker approach to Christian Thinking . . . to young friends," speech transcript, February 1956, Hodgson Papers, box 5, folder 13.

18. Hodgson acknowledged the tension. He planned to write a memoir about his "intellectual experience." See "Statement of my publications . . . ," February 16, 1968, CST, box 5, folder 6.

19. The argument about mysticism is tried out for the first time in an essay titled "The Outlook on Mysticism" for the University of Colorado Men's Essay Club, February 23, 1941. In this instance, Hodgson interpreted mysticism as a revolt against materialism. Hodgson Papers, box 11, folder 1.

20. On Sufism, see Hodgson Papers, box 5, folder 9. On "Mystics," see Hodgson Papers, box 5, folder 7.

21. David M. Hays, "World War II & Equal Rights at the University of Colorado," *Remembrance, Pacific Historic Parks* (2016), http://remembrance.pacifichistoricparks.org/2016/06/24/world-war-ii-equal-rights-at-the-university-of-colorado-1942-1945/.

22. By 1944 he had a book-length list of essays in mind; see the note dated June 29, 1944, Hodgson Papers, box 11, folder 1.

23. "A Plea to the Church," April 27, 1942, Hodgson Papers, box 11, folder 1.

24. Typed note dated May 14, 1942, Hodgson Papers, box 11, folder 1.

25. Typed note dated May 7, 1942, Hodgson Papers, box 11, folder 1.

26. Martin Luther King, Jr., "'Pilgrimage to Nonviolence,' Chicago, Ill., 13 April 1960," http://kinginstitute-stanford-edu.proxy.uchicago.edu/king-papers/documents/pilgrimage-nonviolence.

27. "Speaking of a new world religion, as the Bahhaiists do . . . a plea for the fellowship of religions, for which he saw signs everywhere," September 1942. Also mentioned: Albert

Schweitzer, Toyohiko Kagawa, and Sean Lester. Typed note dated May 7, 1942, Hodgson Papers, box 11, folder 1.

28. Typed note dated May 7, 1942, Hodgson Papers, box 11, folder 1.

29. "For a Pacifist Police Force," August 17, 1942. See also "Deposition concerning Pacifist Discipline Here and Particularly in Reference to myself" (with handwritten marginalia: "For a Pacifist Police Force"), August 14, 1942. Hodgson Papers, box 11, folder 1. Fifty years later this strategy found its theorists: Margaret E. Keck and Kathryn Sikkink, *Activists beyond Borders: Advocacy Networks in International Politics* (Ithaca, NY: Cornell University Press, 1998).

30. "Towards a historical approach to nonviolence," October 1942; "I disagree with Marxism on three points," typed note [1942]; Hodgson Papers, box 11, folder 1.

31. See, e.g., Or Rosenboim, *The Emergence of Globalism: Visions of World Order in Britain and the United States, 1939–1950* (Princeton, NJ: Princeton University Press, 2017).

32. Hodgson, "World History and a World Outlook," in *Rethinking*, 298.

33. "Note on the next revolution . . . ," December 22, 1942, Hodgson Papers, box 11, folder 1.

34. "Defects in Society," typed note of May 8, 1942, Hodgson Papers, box 11, folder 1.

35. Hodgson to "George," June 6, 1942, Hodgson Papers, box 6, folder 21.

36. "Prophetic history," handwritten note dated August 8, 1952, distinguishes three forms of history: (1) creative cooperation among specialists; (2) history designed for the public, answering public questions; (3) "history as expression of vision as effective[ly] as poetry but with impeccable scholarship"; Hodgson Papers, box 6, folder 13.

37. See "The Historian as Theologian," 1967, Hodgson Papers, box 1, folder 18.

38. "Historical Light on the Ideologies from the Religions," 45/46, final March 11, 1946, Hodgson Papers, box 6, folder 13. See also, from ten years later, "The career of the great religions," June 21, 1955, Hodgson Papers, box 6, folder 21.

39. "Toward a Course in World History," February 10, 1949, Hodgson Papers, box 6, folder 21.

40. William H. McNeill, *The Pursuit of Truth: A Historian's Memoir* (Lexington: University Press of Kentucky, 2005).

41. In a confessional note, Hodgson to Charles Long, [1966]: "My thinking has been very Pauline [kerygmatic] for a long time. In principle it ought to be more Johannine [apocalyptic] than Pauline"; Hodgson Papers, box 6, folder 6.

42. For Hodgson's dream book, "Valley of Vision," see Hodgson Papers, box 10, folder 7. Lydia Kiesling, "The Life of Marshall Hodgson," *New York Times Sunday Magazine*, September 10, 2016.

43. See Hodgson's reading list between 1943 and 1946, Hodgson Papers, box 9, folder 9.

44. See Hodgson's notes on Vico, Hodgson Papers, box 6, folder 12; on Rickert, Hodgson Papers, box 6, folder 11.

45. See Hodgson Papers, box 6, folder 22.

46. Hodgson, "World History and a World Outlook"; Hodgson, "A Global Outlook for Christians," *Friends' Intelligencer*, October 20, 1945.

47. Hodgson, "World History and a World Outlook," 298.

48. Hodgson, "A Global Outlook for Christians," 667–68, quote on 667.

49. Hodgson, "World History and a World Outlook," 301.

50. Ibid., 298–99.

51. Ibid.

52. Hodgson, "Hemispheric Inter-regional History," 721–23.

53. Hodgson, "A Global Outlook for Christians," 668.

54. "Outline of a book combatting Western Provincialism," June 23, 1945, Hodgson Papers, box 15, folder 6.

55. "Distortions in World History, 1946–1955," Hodgson Papers, box 6, folder 23.

56. Ibid.

57. Hodgson, "World History and a World Outlook," 300–301. The quotation marks are in the original. Edmund Burke, "There Is No Orient: Hodgson and Said," *Review of Middle East Studies* 44, no. 1 (2010): 13–18.

58. Hodgson, "World History and a World Outlook," 301.

59. On McNeill and Braudel, see Manuel Borutta, "Braudel in Algier: Die kolonialen Wurzeln der 'Méditeranée' und der 'Spatial Turn,'" *Historische Zeitschrift* 303, no. 1 (2016): 1–38. For Hodgson's critique of McNeill, see his lecture "The Sixteenth Century as a Classical Age in Islamdom," April 23, 1964, Hodgson Papers, box 1, folder 4.

60. A view associated with Sanjay Subrahmanyam, "Connected Histories: Notes toward a Reconfiguration of Early Modern Eurasia," in *Beyond Binary Histories: Re-imagining Eurasia to c. 1830*, ed. Victor Lieberman (Ann Arbor: University of Michigan Press, 1999), 289–316.

61. Hodgson, "World History and a World Outlook," 300.

62. "Outline of a book combatting Western Provincialism," June 23, 1945, Hodgson Papers, box 15, folder 6.

63. "Projects," handwritten [in Frankfurt], August 18, 1952. A more academically focused Mercator project is outlined in a handwritten note "To write," October 31, 1954. Hodgson Papers, box 15, folder 6.

64. Outline for a "Handbook of World History," handwritten, January 16–26, 1945, 7, Hodgson Papers, box 15, folder 6.

65. Robert L. Tsai, *America's Forgotten Constitutions: Defiant Visions of Power and Community* (Cambridge, MA: Harvard University Press, 2014), 186–217; Daniel Gorman, "International Law and the International Thought of Quincy Wright, 1918–1945," *Diplomatic History* (2016), https://doi.org/10.1093/dh/dhw052.

66. "Statement of my publications . . . ," February 16, 1968, CST, box 5, folder 4.

67. "Suggestions of problems that might engage my attention under the Committee on Social Thought," [1947–49], typescript, Hodgson Papers, box 15, folder 6.

68. "A proposal to review the treatment of the Orient in the Encyclopedia Britannica," [1954], Hodgson Papers, box 6, folder 23.

69. Marshall G. S. Hodgson, "World History: Toning Down Its 'Western Accent,'" *UNESCO Courier* 7, no. 7 (1954): 24–25; Hodgson, "In the Centre of the Map," *UNESCO Courier* 22, no. 8/9 (1969): 54–55.

70. Edward W. Said, *Orientalism* (New York: Pantheon Books, 1978); Vasant Kaiwar, *The Postcolonial Orient: The Politics of Difference and the Project of Provincialising Europe* (Leiden: Brill, 2014).

71. Hodgson, "Hemispheric Inter-regional History," 723.

72. In this context it is intriguing to reread Dipesh Chakrabarty, *Provincializing Europe: Postcolonial Thought and Historical Difference* (Princeton, NJ: Princeton University Press, 2000).

73. "Central points in critical pluralism," n.d., Hodgson Papers, box 15, folder 6.

74. On the fate of "Islam in Modern Eurasia," see Hodgson Papers, box 15, folders 5 and 11.

75. Alfred Louis Kroeber, *The Ancient Oikoumenê as an Historic Culture Aggregate*, Huxley memorial lecture for 1945 (London: Royal Anthropological Institute of Great Britain and Ireland, 1945). Hodgson to Kroeber, May 21, 1954, Hodgson Papers, box 15, folder 8.

76. Paul Betts, "Humanity's New Heritage: UNESCO and the Rewriting of World History," *Past & Present* 228, no. 1 (2015): 249–85.

77. Louis Gottschalk to Hodgson, September 9, 1953, Hodgson Papers, box 15, folder 8.

78. See the extensive discussions with Milton Singer in the Milton Singer Papers, box 126, folder 6, Special Collections Research Center, University of Chicago Library.

79. Katja Naumann, "Laboratorien der Weltgeschichtsschreibung: Lehre und Forschung an den Universitäten Chicago, Columbia und Harvard von 1918 bis 1968" (Dr. phil., Universät Leipzig, 2012).

80. W. T. Laprade (managing editor of *South Atlantic Quarterly*) to Hodgson, July 30, 1953; François Crouzet to Hodgson, December 12, 1953; Guy Métraux to Hodgson, January 26, 1954; Hodgson Papers, box 15, folder 8.

81. Note on *Cahiers d'histoire mondiale* 1.1 (1954), n.d., Hodgson Papers, box 6, folder 22.

82. Louis Gottschalk, Loren C. MacKinney, and Earl H. Pritchard, eds., *The Foundations of the Modern World [1300–1775]*, Scientific and Cultural History of Mankind 4 (London: Allen & Unwin, 1969).

83. Marshall G. S. Hodgson, "The Unity of Later Islamic History," *Journal of World History* 5 (1960): 879–914.

84. Edward D'Arms to Hodgson, December 1, 1954, Hodgson Papers, box 15, folder 8. Edward D'Arms taught at the University of Colorado in 1942 and may have known (of) Hodgson (courtesy of David M. Hays, University Libraries, University of Colorado Boulder). The powerful John Marshall, D'Arms's superior, considered the idea "most suggestive." John Marshall to Hodgson, November 9, 1954. Hodgson Papers, box 15, folder 8.

85. Kroeber, *Ancient Oikoumenê*.

86. Invitation to a seminar titled Problems in the Development and Interrelations of the Eurasian Civilizations, fall term 1957, Hodgson Papers, box 1, folder 3.

87. Hodgson, "Hemispheric Inter-regional History," 717.

88. Ibid., 716.

89. For clarification of this point, see Hodgson, "The Inter-relations of Societies in History."

90. A first version: "Islam in World History," *UNESCO Courier* 11, no. 2 (1958): 18–21. A last, posthumous version: "The Role of Islam in World History," *International Journal of Middle East Studies* 1, no. 2 (1970): 99–123.

91. Shahab Ahmed, *What Is Islam? The Importance of Being Islamic* (Princeton, NJ: Princeton University Press, 2016).

92. Again, more explicit in Hodgson, "The Inter-relations of Societies in History."

93. The absence of readings on any one (English, German, Swedish) of the European protagonists of geopolitics in Hodgson's archive is striking.

94. Henry A. Winkler (AHR) to Hodgson, November 5, 1965, with a devastating critique of "The Role of Islam in World History," Hodgson Papers, box 15, folder 11.

95. Hodgson, "Hemispheric Inter-regional History," 723.

96. "Central points in critical pluralism," n.d., Hodgson Papers, box 15, folder 6.

97. Hodgson, "Hemispheric Inter-regional History," 717.

98. Draft for abstract for "The Inter-relations of Societies in History," Hodgson Papers, box 11, folder 7.

99. Response to Charles Adams on relations of Islamic studies to the history of religions at the Chicago history of religions conference, October 10, 1965, Hodgson Papers, box 1, folder 16.

100. The entire draft of "The Unity of World History" is in Hodgson Papers, box 14, folder 14, and box 15, folders 1–3. Selected chapters on methodology (minus a fierce critique of Toynbee and a concluding outline) are in Hodgson, *Rethinking.*

101. Marshall G. S. Hodgson, "Modernity and Islamic Heritage," *Islamic Studies* 1, no. 2 (1962): 89–129.

102. See Hodgson Papers, box 7, folder 19, Modern Middle East, 1955–1958; box 7, folder 22, Iran, 1963–1965; box 8, folder 5, Modern Egypt, 1949–1967; box 8, folder 4, Turkey and Turkish nationalism, 1958–1963.

103. The term was coined by Edmund Husserl, *Die Krisis der europäischen Wissenschaften und die transcendentale Phänomenologie: Eine Einleitung in die phänomenologische Philosophie*, Phénoménologie. Mélanges ([Belgrade, 1936]).

104. The notion of "genius" is adapted from A. L. Kroeber, *Configurations of Culture Growth* (Berkeley: University of California Press, 1944).

105. Note on causation in history, December 16, 1962, and August 1963, Hodgson Papers, box 6, folder 26.

106. Untitled text, [1968], CST, box 5, folder 6.

107. "Von G[runebaum] and me and My History . . . ," July 19, 1955, Hodgson Papers, box 6, folder 17.

108. Marshall G. S. Hodgson, "A Comparison of Islam and Christianity as Framework for Religious Life," *Diogenes* 8, no. 32 (1960): 49–79. Hodgson felt rightly that "the English text was mangled in edition." "Publications of Marshall G. S. Hodgson," March 15, 1968, CST, box 5, folder 4. He added a lengthy introduction to correct the editorial mistreatment in *A Comparison of Islâm and Christianity as Frameworks for Religious Life*, University of Chicago Committee on Southern Asian Studies Reprint Series 10 (Chicago: University of Chicago Press, 1960).

109. Lecture notes, April 1968, Hodgson Papers, box 10, folder 20.

110. The most extensive comments and notes on the global condition can be found in the drafts for the twentieth-century chapters of *The Venture of Islam*, Hodgson Papers, box 14, folders 12 and 13.

111. Ibid.

112. Alfred B. Mason (class of 1938) to Hodgson, October 26, 1967, Hodgson Papers, box 3, folder 5.

113. Suffice it to say that this is the same *interrelational* conjuncture, which Charles Bright and I see as the moment at which a "global condition" took shape. Charles Bright and Michael Geyer, "For a Unified History of the World in the Twentieth Century," *Radical History Review* 39 (1987): 69–91.

114. Kenneth Pomeranz, *The Great Divergence: Europe, China, and the Making of the Modern World Economy* (Princeton, NJ: Princeton University Press, 2000).

115. See reference of chapter draft "From Oikoumene to Global European World Order," Hodgson Papers, box 15, folder 3.

116. "The next civilization," handwritten text, July 24, 1952, Hodgson Papers, box 15, folder 6.

117. "Central points in critical pluralism," n.d., Hodgson Papers, box 15, folder 6.

118. "Requirements for and outlines of a History of the Human World," July 3, 1955, Hodgson Papers, box 6, folder 17.

119. "Responsibilities of the historical profession," February 21–28, 1954, Hodgson Papers, box 11, folder 3. See also the note "Is history . . . the study of moral significance of great events?," May 11, 1963, Hodgson Papers, box 6, folder 11.

120. "The next civilization," handwritten text, July 24, 1952, Hodgson Papers, box 15, folder 6.

121. For Hodgson there was no question: "God the creator is not really a god of nature, but of history (hence God creates through Logos!)"; note, [ca. 1965], Hodgson Papers, box 6, folder 6.

CHAPTER SIX

Decentering World History

MARSHALL HODGSON AND THE UNESCO PROJECT

Katja Naumann

Marshall Hodgson and the University of Chicago

Today best known as the author of *The Venture of Islam: Conscience and History in a World Civilization* (Chicago, 1974), Marshall G. S. Hodgson received his BA from the University of Colorado in 1953 with a joint major in economics and political science. While still an undergraduate at Colorado he had been interested in devising approaches to world history that differed from civilization-based ones. He decided to do graduate work in what was then called "medieval Islamic history" with particular focus on Shiʿism and Persian-inflected Islamic culture seen in a global perspective. To this end he enrolled in the Department of Oriental Languages and the interdisciplinary Committee on Social Thought at the University of Chicago. Gustave von Grunebaum became his supervisor in Near Eastern studies, assisted by intellectual historian Muhsin Mahdi. He embarked upon two research projects, the first of which would lead to his dissertation and first book (1955) on the Order of Assassins, the second an article that might have become the basis for a second book on how the early Shiʿa became sectarian.[1] What differentiated Hodgson from his contemporaries was that in addition to committing himself wholeheartedly to becoming an orientalist and historian of Islamic civilization, he was also eager to engage with world history. The essay is primarily about the latter aspect of Hodgson's intellectual legacy. This aspect of his thought developed in Chicago-based and international ventures.

In the early 1950s the University of Chicago was an emerging center for new approaches to world history in the United States. The undergraduate curriculum underwent a process of rethinking. Parallel to the establishment of a radical general education program, under the presidency of Robert M. Hutchins

(1929–1945), which saw the replacement of a history course by discussions of "Great Books" of Western thought and later the establishment of a "Western Civilization" course, efforts were made include non-European history, leading in the 1950s to the establishment of a series of three survey courses introducing students to the history of Indian, Chinese, and Islamic civilizations. The latter was conceived and taught by Hodgson. Related to the College curriculum debates, the Committee on Social Thought (CST) became a nucleus for the conceptual reflection toward interrelated and comparative histories that had emerged in Chicago. Soon after the CST's founding it turned into a place between those collaborators who searched for historical principles in the "Great Books" and through metaphysical reflection and those interested in interdisciplinary comparison of cultures. The collision of strong viewpoints ensured that in and around the CST a lively discussion emerged in which universalist and Eurocentric accounts were subject to withering criticism and a new kind of historical sociology and world history was encouraged. A special role was played by the collaborative project "Intercultural Studies," led by Robert Redfield. The long-term project brought together a group of area studies specialists, anthropologists and sociologists, and historians who developed and tried out methodologies of cross-cultural comparisons. The regular meetings of the study group "Interregional and Intercultural Comparison and Interrelations," including Marshall Hodgson and William McNeill, turned into a lively and steady debate on how to overcome universalist and Eurocentric accounts of the world's past.

With the CST and other schools and institutes, the University of Chicago became a place at which the shape of world-historical studies and alternatives to the universalist-metaphysical concepts of world history were debated and reformulated.[2] The CST was also the perfect place for Marshall Hodgson. Once he was admitted to graduate studies at Chicago, the committee became his institutional anchor, a stable platform from which he could move out into other intellectual arenas. This is where Hodgson did his graduate work, was a professor, and starting in 1965, served as chair. Hodgson's involvement with the CST and Robert Redfield and Milton Singer's "Intercultural Studies" did much to shape his approach to world history. We know relatively more about this aspect of his training. Less well known is Hodgson's participation in the UNESCO-sponsored Scientific and Cultural History of Mankind, which is the subject of this essay.

It was as a student of history and oriental studies at the University of Chicago in the mid-1940s that Marshall Hodgson developed his concern with a decentered and globalized as well as empirically based world history.[3] It remained the central focus of his scholarly work, later becoming intertwined with international efforts in developing new world-historical narratives. "The temptation not only to put one's own land in the center of the map, but one's own people in the center of history, seems to be universal."[4] When Hodgson wrote these lines in 1956 in the *UNESCO Courier* he had been working over a decade on a new kind of world history, which would neither reproduce "centric" narratives, especially where Europe was in the center stage, nor assume that all cross-cultural influence went from West to East. "Let us be frank about it," he noted in his first outline at the age of nineteen, "and stop talking about *world* history, or *general* history, when we really mean the European countries and their colonies."[5] Any proper history of mankind in his view needed to break down ethnocentrism and to unhook from diffusion theories in terms of cultural contact, with their assumed dichotomies and hierarchies between peoples, as "no region or period of human life has, in the long run, been so isolated that it has not had its effects in turn on the rest of us."[6] He was convinced of the necessity of resituating the history of Islamic civilization in a world-historical context, and his 1963 essay "The Inter-relations of Societies in History" summarizes the elements of his alternative to the established civilizational approach to human history.[7]

For Hodgson, metaphysical reasoning about the unity of the world was obsolete, and he endorsed fully its replacement with real historical correlations. One needs "to construct a new sort of world on new lines . . . which shall be genuinely world-wide, but yet free of the *a priori* system-formation associated with the improper sort of 'philosophy of history.' "[8] One aspect of this new orientation was a critique of the traditional historical comparisons, the selected units of analysis and chosen contexts. The only proper ground for making comparisons is the unity of history; that is, "above all interdependence, in ages and regions, in terms of problems posed [. . .] rather than of the human action taken to solve them—the materialist historian's unity from below rather than the idealist's unity from above."[9] We will return to other aspects of his concept for a decentered and nonphilosophical world history.

Characteristically Hodgson's conceptual and historiographical agenda also aimed at reforming historical studies and academic structures in general. As a start he sought to confirm the study of "non-Western" history as an area of professional historical scholarship by grounding it in a thorough consultation of original sources and, by that, situating the subject in its global context. Professionalizing and globalizing non-European history would at the same time enable a historian to resituate Europe and the West in large-scale constellation and from there to rewrite the European past. Such a reorientation required overcoming the separation between systematic disciplines in search of universal knowledge and regional/area studies providing them with material and color. Along this line he strongly argued against the separation of academic departments devoted to philological studies and omitting history, and the area studies centers, which include the past, but only the recent past.

Such an institutional arrangement, he believed, hindered the serious study of civilizations. Instead, philological, archaeological, area studies, and civilization studies for each region or culture of the world should be given its own department where small faculty groups would draw up areas and programs of study, which they would teach on the basis of a shared set of questions and methods. Thus the philologically determined "oriental studies" field could be turned into civilizational studies, a field which would include the European heritage along with the others based on the understanding that historical developments are interrelated and cross-regional in scope. For Hodgson it seemed "absurd for scholars with Islamic studies to be sharing conferences with those in Chinese studies more readily than with those in Medieval European studies" because the clustering could only be justified with a lacking world-historical framing.[10] He was well aware that the reforms of the established regional disciplines he had in mind would be difficult to achieve, but at least, so his hope, centers for civilization studies could be established (alongside the existing "area studies centers") in which new approaches to regional histories and new ones to world histories could be worked out and integrated.[11] With this brief presentation of Hodgson's intellectual and political program of decentering world history, and of freeing from vocabularies, taxonomies, and theories from philosophy what I would like to do in the following parts of the chapter is to situate his work in the international debate over world history in the 1950s and 1960s.

· International Collective Efforts toward Non-Eurocentric World Histories

In the aftermath of World War II, French, British, and US-American historians and educators launched an initiative to devise a more adequate and less Eurocentric history of humanity.[12] Under the auspices of UNESCO, historians and intellectuals from Africa and Asia (just then shaking off the constraints of colonialism) joined in. They were joined by scholars from the Soviet Union and Eastern Europe who had their own project of developing a history of humanity. Although the older Enlightenment-style universal history continued to exist—volumes of Arnold Toynbee's *A Study of History* (1943–61) were still appearing—they aimed at creating a new, more fully global world history.

The change in world order after the end of World War II together with the accelerating processes of decolonization and the ideological rivalries of the global "Cold War" triggered interest in decentering the historicization of the world's past. This occurred not only in Chicago but globally. All around the world one notes efforts toward a new historical narrative. It was spurred on by an ever-louder criticism of older Eurocentric orientations and the demand for the inclusion of the Near East and Far East, Latin America, and Africa. This intellectual dynamic had two dimensions. First, the discovery of the non-Western world as a topic of historians' deliberations occurred in the context of a new intellectual configurations linked to the emergence of area studies. Second, the period was marked by the encounter at a series of international conferences between European and American historians and those from newly independent countries.

In the early 1950s several projects for a new and timely world history were already emerging, inspired by Nehru's *Glimpses of World History* (1934).[13] Alongside those pursued by single scholars were collective endeavors aiming at multiauthored publications. The inclusion of non-European regions implied mastering extensive material and required respective expertise. In this context, two collective projects are especially worthy of mention: the six-volume UNESCO-sponsored Scientific and Cultural History of Mankind (1951–75) and the Soviet Academy of Sciences ten-volume series Vsemirnaja Istoria (World History), which appeared *between* 1955 and 1965. These projects were interrelated. Each sharpened its own approach by critiquing and commenting upon the other. Given the Cold War context and its oppositional character, this is not surprising.

Both projects are relevant here since Marshall Hodgson actively participated in the UNESCO world history and responded to the Soviet history. One way he did so was by distinguishing what he called "pre-commitments," that is, different images of the world, the Christian/Judeo-Christian, the Marxist, the Westernist, and the "four-region pattern." The critical discussion of the flaws, especially of the Westernist type, are not marginal notes or a rhetorical setting for his own ideas. The concept of pre-commitments (today we might say "lenses") was Hodgson's way of organizing the principal options available to world historians in the 1950s and 1960s, which both identified the lenses through world histories were written and allowed him to situate himself in that dynamic field.

In 1951, the General Assembly of UNESCO authorized the edition of a Scientific and Cultural History of Mankind (SCHM) by an international commission contracted and financed by itself. The content of its six volumes had been worked out previously.[14] Already in 1949, French historian Lucien Febvre had been invited to draft an outline for a new history of mankind that would replace the older philosophically informed universal histories. Many of his initial thoughts proved difficult to realize. Febvre's plea to center the books on the "great stages of interchange and borrowing," in order to trace transcultural exchanges and transfers across time, was hard to implement. As work progressed, this suggestion for the main theme was increasingly narrowed down.[15] It began with Febvre's suggestion that they focus on "everything that circulated from one group to the other" to show that humanity has been "constantly shifting about in an endless series of transcontinental migrations" and that any "partitioning of the world is nothing but a fiction." In the end the thematic structure of the volumes was undermined by the emergence of a regional division that treated each region of the world separately. There is, however, a second side to the SCHM. By the time the work was finished, over three hundred scholars, educational experts, and politicians from more than fifty countries had been involved. In this respect, Febvre's prerequisite of a collective study with the largest possible involvement of scholars and scholarly organizations from around the world to accumulate the knowledge needed for a truly global historical exploration was largely met, and the broad collaboration among the authors was consequential.[16]

After the declarations of independence in Asia and Africa during the 1950s, membership in UNESCO increased, and along with it association with the SCHM, since all members of UNESCO had the right to participate and were invited to; many did so. This changed the balance of power, diversified the expectations, and brought about a more global orientation. The attention on the North-South divide noticeably gained priority over the East-West conflict. In a constellation where agents from all regions of the world brought in their views—not sporadically but in an ongoing institutionalized debate—the result could not but shatter consolidated narratives and epistemological certainties. Above all, Eurocentric views were explicitly and persistently challenged, not by single voices but by a collective. In addition, the intellectual context was enriched by the competition between the Soviet and US-American participants, who constantly used the charge of Eurocentrism to justify their viewpoints and to win the hearts and minds of the other side. They could do so because this criticism had become the central theme in the interventions from non-European scholars. The latter were insistent upon the need to obstruct the emergence of a world history ignorant of the histories of large parts of the world.[17] Scholars like Hodgson whose prime expertise was in non-European history constituted an important additional non-Western historical perspective.

One place to observe the influence of both groups is in volume 4 of SCHM, *The Foundations of the Modern World, 1300–1775*. It was assigned to Louis Gottschalk, of the University of Chicago. The associate author-editors were Loren C. MacKinney, professor of medieval history at the University of North Carolina, and E. H. Pritchard, associate professor for Asian history at the University of Chicago. They were joined by Marshall Hodgson, who played a decisive role behind the scenes in the drafting of this volume.

Soon after the final plan for the SCHM was approved in 1952, Gottschalk became worried that adopting a global perspective would require him to have historical knowledge about world regions with which he, as a historian on the French Revolution, was neither familiar nor likely to be in the short run. After all, he intended to narrate the developments of almost five hundred years by starting in the Mediterranean region to go on to the Baltic, thence to the Middle East and Asia, and then Africa and Latin America before returning to Europe.[18] In the call for submissions to the volume in 1953 and 1954 he repeatedly requested articles on specified topics written by area experts to be published in the journal *Cahiers d'histoire mondiale* that would help him to obtain needed information.[19] But the more submissions Gottschalk received the more he began to notice a fundamental problem, namely that much of the available literature on non-European world regions was written from a European or American point of view, while "we know so little about what the world looked like to non-Europeans before the great discoveries. What did the Chinese, Japanese, Arabs, Aztecs, etc. know of each other, of the Pacific islands, of the West, etc. before 1500?"[20]

To counter this imbalance, he tried hard to incorporate criticisms from scholars outside of "Western" academia, of which he received a lot. In 1954, for example, Silvio Zavala (at the time professor at the Centro de Estudios Históricos de El Colegio de México) found the description of the melting together of people of Indian and European origin in Latin America (*mestizaje*) to be unconvincing since it underestimated the extent to which indigenous peoples actually shaped the patterns of the emerging culture.[21] In response to the revised second draft, the eminent Indian historian Ramesh Chandra Majumdar, strongly opposed the parts on South Asia as they reminded one "of the propaganda leaflets written by the Christian missionaries in India about a century ago."[22] Chinese historian Kwok B. Chan remarked that many aspects of Chinese culture were rendered almost meaningless because they were inserted into a European-oriented periodization, regional conception, and topical structure. Constantine K. Zurayk (Zureiq), a Syrian historian, and Mahmud Zayid (Cairo University) objected to the passages on the Islamic world.[23]

From the beginning Gottschalk sought to engage doctoral students and younger scholars at his university who were doing original research on non-European history—not just as sources of information, but also as authors. In the end, the section on Islamic history was written in large part by Marshall Hodgson;[24] those on Indian history were penned by Earl H. Pritchard. Later on, J. A. B. van Buitenen, then associate professor of South Asian languages and cultures at the University of Chicago, also became involved.[25]

So great was the number of critical remarks, Gottschalk and his collaborators soon found they were unable to consider all of them. The second edition alone was sent to several hundred scholars around the world with the request for comment and correction. By the second half of 1958, about 188 pages of responses from historians of fourteen countries, as well as four dozen annotations from corresponding members of the project had been received. By the time the final manuscript was finally sent to print an additional sixty statements had been received.

Although the diversity of criticisms raised caused immense frustration and disappointment, they proved to be productive in the end. In the course of the editing process, a number of important conceptual insights on how to write world history arose. The core problem was identified less in the integration of so many disparate comments as in the problematic character of an objective and undisputable history of mankind, that is, the traditional universalistic ambition of world histories. Increasingly, Gottschalk and his colleagues felt that the diverging viewpoints could be reconciled only to a limited degree. The actual challenge of their endeavor would be to let difference stand rather than to dissolve it. In Gottschalk's words: "[If] conflicts of interpretation cannot be resolved by communication among their conflicting authors, the proper way to proceed, I think, would be to let the conflict stand unresolved. To give the impression that all historical interpretation can be reconciled at the present stage of the world's culture would be, in my judgment, unhistorical."[26] In this fashion he expressed a thoroughly transformed understanding of the craft of writing of world history, one in which it is seen as a field of debate rather than the ground from which a potentially authoritative interpretation can arise.

Following these exchanges, Gottschalk began to address the discrepancy between the omnipresent nominal plea for giving non-Western history a proper place in world-historical narratives and the inadequacy of the existing intellectual efforts and tools for that effort. Along the way he came to doubt that a complete representation of the past and an equal treatment of the developments of all parts of the world would lead to a non-European picture. To the contrary, such an approach could easily turn into a battle over the relative numbers of pages devoted to each of the respective world regions.[27] What was needed instead, he came to believe, was for scholars from or researching Africa, Asia, Latin America, or the Middle East to collaborate in the study of the influences, connections, and exchanges.

Debates about Eurocentrism occurred not only with regard to volume 4, but pervaded the work of the other volumes, too. They stirred a process of negotiation of contents and interpretations, which led to an in-depth questioning of the initial conceptual framework and theoretical assumptions of the SCHM, which yielded three conceptual shifts. First, a reflection of the highly normative nature of various widespread terms set in. In 1955, for example, Gottschalk as the chairman of the committee of author-editors, pointed out that, that the term "Indian Mutiny" (the Indian rebellion against the British in 1857) would be less acceptable in India than in England or the United States.[28] The same thing occurred with regard to the terms "underdeveloped" and "bureaucracy." Even seemingly innocent geographical designations like "Africa" or the "Middle East" were challenged, thus calling into question the very terminology of world regional studies. The initial idea of coming up with a list of "politically correct" terms was rejected, but all authors were asked to indicate in their texts why they employed their particular terminology and why.[29] It became abundantly evident to all the participants that the addition of some information on neglected world regions could never overcome a Eurocentric bias. Instead, and again, the collaboration with scholars from non-European countries and original research from these regions came increasingly to be seen as a fundamental prerequisite.

Second, the hope for a unified account of the world's different pasts and the possibility of arriving at an agreed-upon historical narrative disappeared, as did the faith that diverging perspectives could be finally completely integrated and dissolved. Eventually, a number of venues within which contrasting opinions could be debated emerged. They included the UNESCO journal

Cahiers d'histoire mondiale, which increasingly became a discussion forum. (It had begun as a place where authors might gain access to authoritative work on special topics and problems.) A second place where conflicting views could be stated was in the footnotes of each volume. There opposite readings could be made accessible to the reader, even if they were not incorporated into the main text. All volumes listed the names of the commentators, and the nature of the most severe objections. Their purpose was to make it clear that SCHM was not the final blueprint for world history, but just a provisional step along the path to such an agreement necessarily linked to its time and prolonged into the future.

Third, with the shattering of the idea of the existence of a one-size-fits-all world history, the traditional universalist conception was abandoned—although not by everyone and sometimes in ambivalent ways. For example, René Maheu, in 1962 acting general director of UNESCO, held fast to the idea of a "universal," but eventually came to conceive of it as contextualized, historicized, and emerging from cross-cultural exchanges between different bodies of knowledge. Thus he stated: "Universality springs not from a unique abstract nature but is being gradually evolved, on the basis of a freely acknowledged diversity, through actual contact and a continuous effort at understanding and cooperation."[30] However, some scholars, such as Caroline F. Ware, coauthor of volume 6, went much further in giving up the universalist illusion: "We are writing in a world full of tensions and of proud and sensitive peoples. And truth and accuracy are not enough because truth does not always improve relations among peoples. . . . There is no consensus to the fullest possible degree on the facts about historical relations of nations and peoples."[31]

Ware's and other similar statements expressed a departure from the belief that one historical paradigm could be applied to all regions of the world without doing injustice to idiosyncratic developments. The idea that if each contributor were responsible for the representation of his or her own culture or country, a balanced historical narrative could be achieved came to be regarded as utopian. Thus more than 411 comments from all over the world (and printed in the footnotes) disapproved of the organizing and epistemological principle of the project. The universalist notion of world history with its Eurocentrism and the belief in an unbiased interpretation, free from any political and cultural baggage, came increasingly to be seen as a myth, a highly problematic one, as this statement shows: "The authors [of volume 6] have wished above all for it to be descriptive, neutral, objective, acceptable to everybody. . . . Perhaps, within the outlook of UNESCO, the authors had to conceive of their task as they have done. But in this case it is UNESCO's own conception, applied to the twentieth century, that must be called into question."[32]

These insights were gained through a process of reflection engendered by unsuccessful efforts to accomplish a world history in the style of former universalism, albeit freed from Eurocentric interpretations. On the way disappointment emerged which raised general questions. It was exactly the "failure" in living up to the original hopes that caused skepticism concerning both the possibility of universalism and brought about awareness that other conceptual approaches, as well as other methodological instruments, might be more appropriate.

Hodgson and the Scientific and Cultural History of Mankind

Taking the above account as background, it is no surprise that Marshall Hodgson became involved in the UNESCO project. His own interest in the whole of mankind's development seen through the interrelatedness of different cultures (and civilizations); and in globalizing and decentering historical narratives paralleled that of the SCHM project. So too did his concern with devising tools for a respective and reflective historiographical practice (which for him began with a critical reconsideration of conventional vocabulary).[33] He also shared some of the gained insights, among others that all viewpoints can never be represented (and in fact are not desirable). In history "a balanced view of the field will only be multiply achieved."[34]

When Hodgson entered the project in about 1954 he believed that the outlines of volumes 1 and 2 had been done "with some approach to interregional balance," and he saw "in vol. III a real advance." He anticipated that the good start "at least in point of proportion" would continue. However, volume 4, which interested him most, seemed to him "radically out of focus," not at all offering an interregional perspective. He got his chance when Gottschalk read his as-yet-unpublished article "Hemispheric Inter-regional History as an Approach to World History."[35] Although agreeing in general to the outlined ideas, Gottschalk doubted that there was enough material on the development of the non-European world to write a world history of the sort Hodgson had in mind. To win him over, Hodgson proposed to produce "a work on the role of the Islam in world historical currents . . . which might persuade Dr. Gottschalk of the feasibility of totally changing his chapter." Added to that Hodgson proposed a new structure of volume 4, although he in the end accepted the structure as outlined and agreed to help on the parts on Islamic history that Gottschalk wanted to include. It is important to note that from the beginning Hodgson was aware of the tension that underlay the SCHM project, namely the impossibility of both focusing upon "the specific structure of interregional history" and providing "a summary of all good things in all nations' heritage."[36] Still, he remained committed and considered the UNESCO project as a crucial event of developing "studies of interregional relevance." In fact, in a letter to Edward F. D'Arms, then associate director of the Humanities Division of the Rockefeller Foundation, he described five channels for developing "interregional oriented world histories": the SCHM being one, the others being (a) the production of monographs, although it "presuppose a lot of groundwork in strictly local conditions," (b) "intercultural studies" setups such as that of Redfield and Singer, (c) "immediate writings of brief interregional world histories" (for classroom use), and (d) teamwork toward one of the sketched enterprises.[37]

Hodgson's own conceptual agenda and proposal for decentering world history went much further than what was planned and done with the UNESCO project, the latter being focused on producing a "non-Eurocentric" narrative, while Hodgson explored the common, that is, the global setting of connected regions and civilizations (the "interrelations between . . . imperfect wholes"). He wanted not only to put all regions in perspective but also to see the whole variety of "historical complexes"—ethnic bodies, states, nations, regions, religions, cultural areas, civilizations, cities, trade networks, interstate constellations, the ecumene, etc.—so to be able to grasp the connections between these different scales of human action and organization as crucial factor for development. For this the "largest units of historical activities isolable short of the world taken as whole" seemed to him most suitable.[38] Hodgson's participation in the Scientific and Cultural History of Mankind—in the planning and writing of volume 4 more specifically, as well as in the articles he wrote for the *Cahiers d'histoire mondiale* and the *UNESCO Courier* contributed to the growing conceptual reflection in the project and displays his ability to conceptualize world history.[39]

Hodgson was an observer of the discussion of the project and debates on world history in general at the International Congresses of Historical Sciences in Stockholm (1960) and Vienna (1965).[40] The Stockholm congress provided a first opportunity to present ongoing reflection and practice of writing world histories. There were presentations by Felix Gilbert and Evgenij M. Zhukov,[41] among others. Several sessions were devoted to it: "Methods of Universal History Writing" and "Evolution and World History" (submitted by the West and East German committees respectively) and a panel titled "World History Writing" proposed by the US-American committee.[42] In the latter, Louis Gottschalk presented on the traditions of world history writing up to the early twentieth century and on the cornerstones of a timely global interpretation—the rejection of the civilizing and Eurocentric position and the support for collective works—which obviously reflected his experiences in the SCHM. In the ensuing debate—over which Erik Molnár (Budapest) presided and to which, among others, László Zsigmond (Budapest), Geoffrey Barraclough (Cambridge), and Jacques Godechot (Toulouse) contributed—the decentering of world history and the integration of non-European history took the form of an imperative. Even Theodor Schieder (Munich), otherwise quite attached to the more philosophical concept of universal history, was able to step back from the national framework fixated on Europe in favor of world regions.[43]

These discussions were triggered not least by the simultaneous work on the Vsemirnaja Istoria v dejati tomach at the Russian Academy of Sciences by Nikolai Lukin (and published between 1955 and 1965). Although conceived shortly after the Russian Revolution, its original sociohistorical perspective had already been replaced by an explicitly Marxist orientation. Upon taking over the project in 1937, Lukin wrote a programmatic paper titled "The Main Problems in Conceptualizing World History." It laid out three guidelines. First, the Vsemirnaja Istoria should depart from Hegelian-style world history and reconstruct actual historic change. Second, the traditional distinction between ancient, medieval, and modern history, plausible only for Western European history, would be replaced with the sequence of social formations (feudalism, capitalism, and socialism) as described in Marxist theory especially focused on social and economic transformation. Third, the work would begin with the emergence of an integrated world at the end of the eighteenth century and the implementation of industrial capitalism, the emergence of world markets, and the emergence also of an international division of labor.[44]

Although the suggested chronology clearly privileged Europe (the medieval age was synonymous with feudalism; the modern era appeared as prehistory of the October Revolution), it already presupposed a fundamental critique of Eurocentrism. This surfaced notably in the denial of a distinction between cultures having a history and other having none. A year later, and shortly before Lukin's arrest, the topics for thirty volumes had been specified and first authors had been found, so that by the beginning of World War II, five volumes were in progress and the one on the French Revolution had been published.

Following the war, the project was continued under the auspices of the Soviet Academy of Science, under the direction of Evgenij M. Zhukov, and its scope was reduced to ten volumes. Now non-European history—which played a major role in Russian historiography from its beginnings, received additional weight. Zhukov had studied Japan at the Department of Near Eastern Languages and Civilizations in Leningrad and in 1941 had been awarded a doctorate in Japanese history from Moscow University. For three years, he worked as a professor of Asian history; shortly thereafter, he took over the leadership of the Pacific Institute (Tichookaanski Institut) at the Academy of Sciences and was named deputy director of the Institute for History there.[45]

Lukin's scholarly expertise played out in the composition of the editorial staff of Vsemirnaja Istoria. Among its twenty-four members, at least four were experts on the non-European world. In addition, there were seven experts on regions in western and southeast Europe, seven historians of Russia, and five researchers from the social sciences.[46] The new design was also revealed in the project's organization. Each volume addressed non-European processes in self-contained chapters, albeit the space dedicated to non-European processes declined in the volumes on the modern era.

In this respect, Zhukov and his colleagues met their aim of countering the Eurocentric interpretations of "bourgeois historiography," in which the "spirit of colonialism" was challenged by an alternative interpretation. Concerning the periodization they were far less successful in holding onto Lukin's scheme. Differing rhythms in the chronology of social formations in world regions were hardly recognized, while the overall Marxist-Leninist framework, in which the global development toward socialism was the master narrative, remained unchallenged. Left unexplained were the vast differences between regions of the world.

However, contrary to the conceptual design that placed the socioeconomic constellations in the foreground, the individual volumes offered a sequence of national and regional histories, identifying the respective class struggles and revolutionary transformations. One could read this as evidence that Soviet world history remained trapped in a typology that reduced the history of mankind to the history of states and thereby marginalized interactions. But Zhukov's claim that he and his colleagues wanted first and foremost to move away from the homogenizing concept of "civilization" must be taken seriously. Their conceptual ambition was to shatter that container. Instead, they wanted to study national history as a precondition for reconstructing transfers and entanglements between societies and nations.

In a panel at the 1960 Stockholm conference on the periodization of world history, Zhukov launched a critique of the category "civilization." He asserted that a civilizations-based history would result in the opposite of universal history because it divided humanity. To advance the unifying aspects and commonalities, he suggested, the first step would be to retrace the specific developments of individual nations. Even then, he claimed, the study of history would be at an early stage because the then-existing world history was incapable of describing the path of all nations. Provisionally, Zhukov concluded, one should hold to the rule that where empirical knowledge on integrative processes is lacking, one should outline national, geographic, and historical particularities instead of assuming uniformity and synchronicity in a deductive manner.[47] This critique must have been heard by those involved in the UNESCO world history project, including Marshall Hodgson.

One can only guess what Hodgson thought about Zhukov's critique. Nonetheless, it is clear that he had a constructivist understanding of civilizations. For him civilizations were "wider groupings of cultures . . . as they share consciously in interdepended cumulative traditions." However defined, he insisted, civilizations "must not be hypostatized, as if [they] had a life independent of its human carriers." Hodgson saw civilizational units as "a function of the inquirer's purpose," so that "what civilizations are singled out is a matter of choice, one among several possible delimitations."[48] For him civilizations were both historically existing cultural formations and valuable analytical tools for studying larger-order interactions and countering Eurocentric views.[49] Ever the pedagogue, Hodgson offered a limited defense of the concept of civilization in a 1957 memo calling for a new University of Chicago course on the history of Russian civilization: "The substitution of *nation* for *civilization* would take away much of the value of a civilization-course and make the study of Russian civilization incomparable with Western civilization, which is studied as a whole (not nation by nation) in the rest of the student's humanistic education."[50]

Conclusion

By the time of his death in 1968, Marshall Hodgson had become a leading figure in developing a more adequate history of humanity. However, as this essay has sought to demonstrate, he was not alone. His project must be viewed as part of a much larger (indeed global) post–World War II intellectual and conceptual effort which had one of its bases at the University of Chicago. Often the effort was also broadly collaborative. Here the UNESCO world history project was crucial. Seen in this context, the role of Hodgson as a leading proponent of a multilayered and multisited reconceptualization of world history comes out clearly.

Attempts to integrate European and non-European history into world history began in the 1950s and 1960s. But the possibility of doing so was undermined by the persistence of fundamental conceptual, political, and ideological disagreements. Given the unresolvable tension between universalist aspirations and diverse human pasts, some historians, and soon even more, began to accept the impossibility of a comprehensive, timeless, and neutral world history. In coming to this realization Hodgson's constructivist, self-reflective, and idiosyncratic thinking has been crucial. His genius remains, but it is enriched by understanding that it was also the work of many hands.

Following the 1989 collapse of the Soviet Union, the "West is Best" narrative reemerged with full force. The search for a more adequate human-centered world history has become more and more difficult, as difficult as the effort to sustain the optimism of the 1980s and early 1990s both in the United States and around the world. This essay presents the beginning of a process of intellectual excavation of the work of an entire generation of world historians who sought to come to terms with and to transcend the limits of traditional universal histories. Perhaps this might be a good moment to reengage with their spirit.

Notes

1. Marshall G. S. Hodgson, *The Order of Assassins: The Struggle of the Early Nizârî Ismâ'îlîs against the Islamic World* ('s Gravenhage: Mouton, 1955); Hodgson, "How Did the Early Shîʿa Become Sectarian?," *Journal of the American Oriental Society* 75, no. 1 (January–March 1955): 1–13.

2. The essay is based on my study *Laboratorien der Weltgeschichtsschreibung: Lehre und Forschung an den Universitäten Chicago, Columbia und Harvard 1918 bis 1968* (Göttingen: Vandenhoeck & Ruprecht, 2018).

3. For one of the earliest outlines, which already contains the cornerstones of his approach to world history, see his unpublished manuscript "Handbook of world citizenship," January 16–26, 1945, in Marshall G. S. Hodgson Papers, box 9, folder List of Suggestions, Special Collections Research Center, University of Chicago Library (hereafter cited as Hodgson Papers).

4. Marshall G. S. Hodgson, "In the Centre of the Map: Nations See Themselves as the Hub of History," *UNESCO Courier*, May 1956, 16–18, republished in Marshall G. S. Hodgson, *Rethinking World History: Essays on Europe, Islam, and World History*, ed. Edmund Burke III (Cambridge: Cambridge University Press, 1993), 29–34.

5. Marshall G. S. Hodgson, "World History and a World Outlook," *Social Studies* 35 (1944): 297–301, republished in Hodgson, *Rethinking*, 35–44, quote on 36.

6. Marshall G. S. Hodgson, "Historical Method in Civilizational Studies," published posthumously as the prologue to *The Venture of Islam: Conscience and History in a World Civilization*, 3 vols. (Chicago: University of Chicago Press, 1974), and republished in Hodgson, *Rethinking*, 72–90, quote on 75.

7. Marshall G. S. Hodgson, "The Inter-relations of Societies in History," *Comparative Studies in Society and History* 5, no. 2 (1963): 227–50.

8. Marshall G. S. Hodgson, "The Objectivity of Large-Scale Historical Inquiry," chapter in unpublished manuscript "The Unity of World History," published in Hodgson, *Rethinking*, 247–66, quote on 249.

9. Marshall G. S. Hodgson, "Conditions of Historical Comparisons among Ages and Regions," chapter in unpublished manuscript "The Unity of World History," published in Hodgson, *Rethinking*, 267–87, quote on 267 and 270.

10. Hodgson, "Historical Method," in *Rethinking*, 82.

11. Such a move he suggested also for his own university and the "Committee on Middle Eastern Studies," which was in his view crippling; see Hodgson to Adams, February 26, 1965, in University of Chicago, Committee on Social Thought, Records, box 3, folder Committee Near East, Special Collections Research Center, University of Chicago Library (hereafter cited as CST).

12. Matthias Middell and Katja Naumann, "The Writing of World History in Europe from the Middle of the Nineteenth Century to the Present: Conceptual Renewal and Challenge to National Histories," in *Transnational Challenges to National History Writing in Europe*, ed. Matthias Middell and Lluis Roura y Aulinas (New York: Palgrave Macmillan, 2013), 54–139; Benedikt Stuchtey and Eckhardt Fuchs, eds., *Writing World History, 1800–2000* (Oxford: Oxford University Press, 2003).

13. Middell and Naumann, "The Writing of World History," 54–139; Stuchtey and Fuchs, *Writing World History*.

14. Until recently, the project was only briefly and negatively noted in the literature. A more appreciative consideration can be found in Poul Duedahl, "Selling Mankind: UNESCO and the Invention of Global History 1945–76," *Journal of World History* 22, no. 1 (2011): 101–33; Paul Betts, "Humanity's New Heritage: UNESCO and the Rewriting of World History," *Past & Present* 228 (2015): 249–85.

15. Report of Lucien Febvre, May 1949, in Scientific and Cultural History of Mankind Papers, box 4, folder 2.111, UNESCO Archives, Paris (hereafter cited as SCHM Papers).

16. The commission started out with 8 members but gradually was enlarged. At the time of its dissolution in 1969, its bureau consisted of 22 members, whose corresponding members numbered 93 scholars from 42 countries. An additional 130 people from roughly 50 countries took part. Three or four author-editors wrote each of the six volumes and most of them had additional collaborators at their disposal.

17. Demands for a more balanced treatment of non-European history were often associated with the effort to have the representation of one's own national perspective accentuated, and thus had markedly nationalistic intentions. Many contributors used their (often recently gained) political sovereignty and membership in UNESCO to demand a strong representation of their national history; see on this aspect Katja Naumann, "Avenues and Confines of Globalizing the Past: UNESCO's International Commission for a Scientific and Cultural History of Mankind (1952–1969)," in *Networking the International System: Global Histories of International Organizations*, ed. Madeleine Herren (Heidelberg: Springer, 2014), 187–200.

18. Plan, in Annual Report, International Commission for a Scientific and Cultural History of Mankind, June 1952, pp. 16–17 and 20–21, in SCHM Papers, box 5, folder 2.114.

19. The *Cahiers d'histoire mondiale*, a UNESCO journal edited by Febvre since 1953, was founded with the intention to be a source of information for the author-editors by publishing research on special topics and by discussing controversial issues. Gottschalk's use of the journal is reflected in the following letters: Métraux to Gottschalk (about an article on world views in various civilizations), May 29, 1953, and Gottschalk to Métraux, March 12, 1954 (about an article on science in Turkey), SCHM Papers, box 32, folder 2.83 (13); Métraux to Hu-Shi, June 2, 1953 (request for information on China before the discoveries), SCHM Papers, box 21, folder 2.629.4.

20. Gottschalk to Métraux, May 20, 1953, SCHM Papers, box 32, folder 2.83 (13). Gottschalk points to his assistant Karl J. Weintraub, then a doctoral student at the University of Chicago, as the one calling his attention to this problem.

21. Silvio Zavala, "Comments on the Introduction to vol. IV," SCHM Papers, box 32, folder 2.83 (13). In response to this issue (January 26, 1954, SCHM Papers, box 32, folder 2.83 [13]), Gottschalk began to discuss with Zavala how the pre-Columbian history in general should be interpreted and periodized. Zavala in turn asked his colleagues Padro Armillas and Juan Coma to develop a chronology that would emphasize the role indigenous America played for the world's development until the discoveries as well as its influence on other world regions. Drawing up the conclusions of a seminar of Mexican historians on these issues (October 1954, Mexico City), they suggested that volume 4 would contain a subchapter titled "Contribution indigène à la culture universelle, vers 1500." Gottschalk complied with this proposal, and although it did not survive the many revisions of the manuscript, he integrated repeatedly passages on non-European world regions written by scholars studying these histories; see "Notes on the Preparation and Editorial Treatment of Volume IV," in Louis Gottschalk, Loren C. MacKinney, and Earl H. Pritchard, eds., *The Foundations of the Modern World*, Scientific and Cultural History of Mankind 4 (London: Allen & Unwin, 1969), xv–xix, and the correspondence between Zavala, Gottschalk, Métraux, and Ralph Turner (October 1954 to July 1955), SCHM Papers, box 20, folder 2.628 (1).

22. Comments about vols. II & IV, Majumdar to Métraux, May 22, 1962, SCHM Papers, box 21, folder 2.629.2.

23. Turner to Carneiro, "Alternative Proposals for Revising vol. IV," SCHM Papers, box 26, folder 2.729. Also C. K. Zyrayk, "Comment on vol. IV," September 1958, SCHM Papers, box 20, folder 2.629.

24. Acknowledgments in the volume, and List of Publications (by Hodgson), CST, folder Hodgson File I.

25. Acknowledgment in the volume, and Gottschalk to Métraux, July 2, 1954, and January 18, 1956, SCHM Papers, box 32, folder 2.83 (13).

26. Gottschalk to Carneiro, July 28, 1964, SCHM Papers, box 32, folder 2.83 (15).

27. Métraux to Gottschalk, June 24, 1955, SCHM Papers, box 32, folder Gottschalk.

28. Gottschalk to Carneiro, March 30, 1955, SCHM Papers, box 28, folder 2.823.

29. The authors of volume 6 decided to address that directly in the preface: "In writing contemporary history, the historian has to make use of terms that are interpreted differently and carry a different emotional weight in different countries and situations—terms such as 'West,' 'East,' 'underdeveloped,' 'totalitarian,' 'democratic,' 'capitalist,' 'communist,' 'socialist,' and even neutral words like 'bureaucracy.' Since it is impossible to avoid such

words or to put a note every time misunderstanding might arise from their use, we must rely on the collaboration of the reader to understand them in the context in which they appear, and to do the same with such imprecise designations of geographical areas as Near East, Middle East, Tropical Africa, Oceania." Caroline F. Ware, J. M. Romein, and K. M. Panikkar, eds., *The Twentieth Century*, Scientific and Cultural History of Mankind 6 (London: Allen & Unwin, 1966), xiv.

30. René Maheu, foreword to Charles Morazé, ed., *The Nineteenth Century, 1775–1905*, Scientific and Cultural History of Mankind 5 (London: Allen & Unwin, 1976), xv.

31. Caroline F. Ware, "The History of the Scientific and Cultural History of Mankind: Some Problems of Interpretation," *Cahiers d'histoire mondiale* 5, no. 1 (1959): 270–92.

32. "Supplement to Author-Editor's Preface," in Ware, Romein, and Panikkar, *The Twentieth Century*, 10n39.

33. Already in his first conceptual note Hodgson shows his discontent with established names and thinks about alternatives (Near East versus Arabistan, and Eurasia as marker for Europe-Arabistan-India). See comment "On Terms: Outlines of World History, 1942," attachment to letter to "George," June 6, 1942, Hodgson Papers, box 12, folder Notes for History of the Human World. Later, and in his typical manner of taking notes, he held that the "Term 'Turkish' is useful (instead) of 'Ottoman' only if one keeps a Eur'n perspective, so that the more easterly Turks can be ignored . . . McNeill uses 'Tatar' for the Crimean Turks + 'Turks' for the Ottoman; the one implying a Russian perspective too"; notes on William McNeill, *Europe's Steppe Frontier, 1500–1800* (1964), p. 5, Hodgson Papers, box 10, folder Eastern Europe.

34. Hodgson, "The Objectivity of Large-Scale Historical Inquiry," 261.

35. Marshall G. S. Hodgson, "Hemispheric Inter-regional History as an Approach to World History," *Cahiers d'histoire mondiale* 1 (1954): 715–23. The article was republished in revised and expanded form as "The Inter-relations of Societies in History," *Comparative Studies in Society and History* 5, no. 2 (1963): 227–50.

36. Hodgson to D'Arms, September 7, 1954, pp. 1–2, Hodgson Papers, box 12, folder Old Oik Pages.

37. Ibid., pp. 3–4.

38. Hodgson, "The Objectivity of Large-Scale Historical Inquiry," 255ff. and 278.

39. Marshall G. S. Hodgson, "The Unity of Later Islamic History," *Cahiers d'histoire mondiale* 5, no. 4 (1960): 879–91; Hodgson, "In the Centre of the Map."

40. See "History of the Committee on Social Thought," CST, box 1, folder CST I, Foundation. Hodgson was a Fulbright scholar at Alighar Muslim University (1951/52), spent a year in Frankfurt with the Chicago-Frankfurt exchange (1952/53), traveled through Turkey and the Middle East with a Rockefeller grant (1956), and served as a visiting professor at the Center for Middle Eastern Studies at Harvard University.

41. Felix Gilbert, "Cultural History and Its Problems," and Evgenij M. Zhukov, "The Periodization of World History," in *Rapports, XIe Congrès International des Sciences Historiques*, vol. 1, *Methodology* (Stockholm: Almqvist & Wiksell, 1960), 40–58 and 74–88.

42. Similar proposals by the Bulgarian, Czech, and Swedish committees were rejected: "Liste des thèmes retenues et des rapports y afférents," Comité International des Sciences Historiques (CISH), AS 105 224, folder Michel François, Archives Nationales de France,

Paris; "Tableau des thèmes de rapports retenue pour le XII CISH, Vienna 1965," CISH, 105 AS 300.

43. For Gottschalk's lecture and the report on the ensuing debate, see *Rapports, XIIe Congrès International des Sciences Historiques*, vol. 4, *Méthodologie et Histoire Contemporaine* (Vienna: Burger, 1965), 5–19, and *Actes, XIIe Congrès International des Sciences Historiques* (Vienna: Burger, 1965), 525–40.

44. "Osnovnye problemy postroeniia vsemirnaoi istorii," *Istorik-marksist* 3 (1937): 3–23.

45. Between 1942 and 1945, Zhukov had also been a member of the Institute for Pacific Relations (IPR), a multinational nongovernmental organization that addressed political, economic, and social processes in the Pacific region, a think tank on American foreign policy that sought to break Europe's geopolitical superiority, but also a network of academic experts. S. L. Tikhvinskii, "Istorik-Enciklopedist, Redaktor, Pedagog k 100-letiiu so dnia rozhdeniia Akademika E. M. Shukowa" [Historian, encyclopedian, editor, professor: At the occasion of the one hundredth anniversary of E. M. Zhukov], *Vestnik Rossiiskoi Akademii Nauk* 77, no. 10 (2007): 911–14. An English translation of this article appeared in *Herald of the Russian Academy of Sciences* 77, no. 5 (2007): 497–500.

46. All area scholars had studied the Near and Far East; scholars with in-depth knowledge of Latin America and Africa were not included in the editorial staff. See Hans Hecker, *Russische Universalgeschichtsschreibung von den "Vierziger Jahren" des 19. Jahrhunderts bis zur sowjetischen "Weltgeschichte"* (1955–65) (Munich: Oldenbourg, 1983), 198–200.

47. *Rapports, XIe Congrès International des Sciences Historiques*, vol. 1, *Methodology* (Stockholm: Almqvist & Wiksell, 1960), 74–88.

48. Hodgson, "Historical Method," in *Rethinking*, 81, 84, 85.

49. Johann P. Arnason, "Marshall Hodgson's Civilizational Analysis of Islam: Theoretical and Comparative Perspectives," in *Islam in Process: Historical and Civilizations Perspectives*, ed. J. P. Arnason, A. Salvatore, and G. Stauth (Bielefeld: Transcript, 2006), 23–47.

50. Hodgson, "Memo on Civilization Courses," December 16, 1957, in Hodgson Papers, box 12, folder Philosophy of Education; see also "A Non-Western Civilization Course in a Liberal Education, with Special Attention to the Case of Islam," *Journal of General Education* 12, no. 1 (1959): S39–49; and *Introduction to Islamic Civilization: Course Syllabus and Selected Readings*, 3 vols. (Chicago: University of Chicago Press, 1958–59).

CHAPTER SEVEN

Military Patronage and Hodgson's Genealogy of State Centralization in Early Modern Eurasia

Pamela Kyle Crossley

Hodgson and the Mongol Political Legacy in Eurasia

It is not entirely mysterious that Marshall Hodgson is usually left out of the intellectual history of Eurasian studies. Many have seen "military patronage"[1] in Hodgson's volumes as ancillary to the notion of gunpowder empires, just a bit of furniture going down with the ship. Yet modern Eurasian history rests very much on concepts that Hodgson linked together under military patronage. One obstacle to establishing the relevance for Eurasia was that Hodgson presented military patronage as peculiar to the Islamic world. This has not proved consonant with what is now known—or now seen—of the history of central Eurasia and China. Despite Hodgson's view of the limitations of his model, the heritage of Eurasian historical studies is substantially deepened with the restoration of military patronage as a foundation discourse in early modern state centralization.

In volume 3 of *The Venture of Islam*, Hodgson places military patronage at the core of the Mongol political legacy (3:16). A ruler was proprietor of the state by virtue of his personal monopoly on military power, and a centralized bureaucracy emerged through abstraction and elaboration of the ruler's ostensible household.[2] His role as military proprietor fixed the ruler as the source of both instructions in particular and legitimacy in general, adumbrating the caliphal persona of the Ottoman emperorship and integrating remnant elements of transcendent Mongol rulership, particularly through the (adapted) Islamic concepts of the *padishah*. Centralization and elevation of rulership above the legitimating powers of the religious hierarchy were, for Hodgson, products of the emergence of new rulerships founded on monopolization of long-range military technologies and personalization of the government as an extension of the ruler himself. These basic premises of Hodgson's treatment of military patronage anticipated ideas that have become salient in Eurasian and world history in the twenty-first century.

What Was the Military Patronage State?

Military patronage was just one variety of patronage as a sociopolitical formation. Hodgson's explanation for the vitality of nomadic patterns of military patronage in the Islamic world rested partly upon his narrative of patronage in Islamic regimes before the arrival of nomadic rule (*Venture* 2:110). Patronage of rural elites was the key to social coherence and cultural development in the countryside and was indispensable to urban society. Extension of the household's patterns of authority, identity, and obligation to local society, landowners, merchants, aristocrats, and religious elites anchored flexible and easily legible systems in which all classes and individuals (whether local or foreign) could be positioned. Early Islamic empires were in Hodgson's view accretions of larger and larger patronage systems, eventually culminating in patronage rooted directly in the official household of the ruler. In the eleventh through the thirteenth centuries, Hodgson suggested, nomadic political regimes of the Eurasian steppe were accustomed to using a cognate pattern of patronage, but based on the primacy of military power rather than on wealth or religious authority. This was a particularly effective pattern of affiliation in a world where territorial connections were fleeting and political alliances were unstable. Patronage legacies, Hodgson found, made steppe nomads easily accommodated in "Islamdom." He saw this as a contrast to China, where nomads appeared to be "unabsorbable" (*Venture* 2:400).

The Turkic slice of Islamdom became the threshold over which the Mongols were ushered into western Eurasia. In contrast to the complex traditional forms of patronage in the earlier Islamic world, the Mongols concentrated primarily upon military patronage and secondarily upon sponsorship of the sources of wealth and prestige, including the arts. The tendencies of steppe rulers to both patronize the arts and look with a select indifference on the religious affiliations of subject populations were linked, though Hodgson could only attribute to the link some kind of "noblesse oblige"—"to protect and patronize whatever of excellence was to be found in the conquered cities . . . including all the arts of luxury and even various spiritual cults" (*Venture* 2:401). Today's scholarship, particularly on architecture, would see this connection in a different light. In the military patronage states of the Turks and Mongols, the arts that in their production most resembled the patterns of military mobilization—for instance, the concentration, command, and reward of ironworkers or goldsmiths, or the building of elaborate edifices—were privileged. In most cases, they were closely tied through the celebration of the warrior ruler (often a personal sponsor of the work); this was often the subject of imperially encouraged poetry and narrative painting, and it was usually explicitly or implicitly signaled through inscriptions on architectural edifices.[3] In Hodgson's model, the Mongols' adherence to steppe priorities, even after their transfer to and commitment to the sedentary zone, caused them to assign a low value to agriculture and common industry. Mongol militarism was inversely related to the broadest economic health of their empires (*Venture* 2:402). I take this to mean that the more energetic and extensive the conquests, the more dire the consequences for agriculture and local trade. On the other hand, the steadier the economic improvement of agriculture and industry, the weaker the conquest enthusiasms of the Mongols and, as a byproduct, their tendency to define themselves narrowly as outsiders and occupiers. Hodgson summarized the agenda yoking economy and the arts to the agenda of the conquest state: "First, a legitimation of independent dynastic law; second, the conception of the whole state as a single military force; third, the attempt to exploit all economic and high-cultural resources as appanages of the chief military families" (*Venture* 2:405).

Self-replicating civil government was not a priority for such regimes, which attained durability—when they did—by relying upon the basic precepts of the steppe and what they could safely import from local political legacies. Dynasticism (particularly among the Chinggisids) and the Yasa of Chinggis (which was first accepted to be a written document in the Islamic lands)[4] were central. But in the Islamic world the existing code of sharia and its attendant institutions of education and adjudication would prove advantageous, particularly when a school of interpretation could legitimate absolutism.[5] Indispensable government functions that had been part of the earlier civil bureaucracy, such as census taking and tax collection, became new functions of the military (*Venture* 2:407). But in Hodgson's view, the history of the Islamic steppe regimes demonstrated that militarization of the state was in itself destabilizing. Dynasticism strengthened the political ambitions of the aristocratic branches of the imperial lineage, while both the Yasa and sharia could be used to legitimate whichever rival individual or lineage could seize power (2:405–8). As a result, these regimes tended toward either fatal political fragmentation at the top or a more gradual dissolution at the bottom produced by attempts by the imperial court to pacify and stabilize the military class—through land grants, religious tolerance, or devolution of political power to the military elites themselves. The Mongol regimes, especially in the Islamic world, where land grants to military elites were common, were put on a knife's edge by the requirements of military patronage—success if grants of wealth and authority created centipede coherence around the court, failure if the same grants frayed the coherence of the regime from the lower military ranks up (2:408–9).

The apparent exceptions to this tendency toward early dissolution among the steppe legacy states were the Ottomans and the "Timurîs" of India (that is, the Mughals). The Safavids, who had no direct steppe legacy but clearly benefited from the Turco-Mongol political model, were also distinguished for longevity. All began with a period of conquest based less upon the quick terrorization and seizure methods of the Mongols and more upon processes of negotiation, rewards, and preservation of the land and markets as sources of wealth. As polities they all showed the effects of the steppe heritage, and they were founded upon the old principle of military patronage—the government was essentially a tool for the transfer of wealth from a producing majority to a ruling minority, using the military to enforce the direction of flow. They all affiliated themselves with Islam early and made effective use of the religious hierarchy to stabilize their rule (*Venture* 2:426–28, 435–37; 3:29–31). By such means these regimes preserved the essential transfer dynamics of military patronage without succumbing to the most destabilizing weaknesses of the earlier Mongol systems. They not only survived long enough to enter the technical age of heavy weapons but were peculiarly well positioned to take advantage of new technologies, since the rulers were wealthy enough and free enough of internal political constraints to make the concentrated investments in mining, manufacturing, training, and deployment to realize rapid advancements in their military—and subsequently diplomatic—ventures (2:426–28, 435–37; 3:29–31).

Hodgson's development of the military patronage model described above is based upon the idea of the imperial household as both the literal and the figurative source of the state. Incorporation into the state was effected as a kind of adoption by the ruler. Patronage here was specific, since the khan/emperor/sultan functioned as the father, or owner, of the state household. The form of subordination implied here is very characteristic of the steppe, and many of its terms are conventionally translated into English as "slave" or "servant" (*Venture* 3:5). Either serves perfectly well to define by contrast the role of the "lord" as the father, protector, and master of his dependents. In such systems, intimacy between the throne and the military forces was expressed by terms suggesting household space. The Janissaries, for instance, were also the *kapıkullan*, or the imperial household guard (literally, the door keepers), and officers sometimes incorporated icons of household service implements in their insignia of office. The notion of "household" meant close connection with, and sometimes direct command by, the emperor or his representative in the imperial lineage. In law and in political rhetoric, the whole military force was figurized as a dependency of the imperial household. The understanding of the state as an extension of the imperial household and its patronage relationships with military elites has been an enduring theme in Mongol and Eurasia studies, though virtually always without reference to Hodgson. Since the "household" conceit is the matrix in which the lord-dependent relationship became the essence of the state, ideas such as those of Hodgson's near contemporaries Joseph F. Fletcher, Jr. (1936–1984)[6] and Michael Cherniavsky (1922–1972)[7] on the effects of a Mongol legacy animating the development of rulership and state in the Ottoman, Russian, and Qing Empires could have been very beneficially connected to the Hodgson model of centralization under military patronage.

Consonant with this institutional expression, rulers saw the state as their personal patrimony. I take Hodgson's comment that the nomadic empires tended to be uninterested in any difference "between public and private" to be an invocation of this legacy (*Venture* 2:402). For the Mongols, the "lord" (*ejen*) of the house is its owner, and his legatees will be lords over their own patrimonies, and so on, into the future. Populations of central and northern Asian empires from a very early period were organized by patrimony, or "estate" (*ordo* and its variants), which in all cases were either gifted by the ruler or legitimated through recognition by the ruler; ownership of dependent populations was legally indistinct from ownership of herds, tents, wagons, weapons, and precious objects. In the case of patrimonial transmission, not only the material goods but also legitimate domination of populations passed from father to son. This equation was so profound in Mongolian tradition that the word for patrimony, *ulus*, became in the thirteenth century the term for the empires—both of the Great Khan at Karakorum and the appanages in China, Central Asia, Iran/Iraq, and Russia—and today is the word for "nation."

The lord was a father, and he was required to feed and shelter his charges. The dependents were minors, who were obliged to honor and obey their protector and benefactor. Abuse of dependents—as contrasted to lawful punishment—was a serious breach of Mongol law, as it had been in earlier steppe law. Accusations of abuse could be used as a device by the ruler to strip elites of their dependent populations, curbing the wealth and power of aristocrats who might challenge the throne. This was an issue consistently seen as distinct from the obligation of the lord to allow his dependents to turn to any religion that did not diminish his own standing. This probably accounts not only for the religious diversity tolerated among Mongol women particularly but also the history of the Il-khans in which common Mongols (all technically dependents of the ruler) were permitted to convert to Islam well before conversion became an issue for the rulers and their households.[8] The values of the lord-dependent relationship may also have accounted to some degree for Mongol religious tolerance. This is a remarkably faint theme in Hodgson's treatment of Mongol-legacy states, possibly because of Hodgson's argument that the Mongols were predisposed toward Islam, or at least toward Islamic states. Modern historians of Eurasia are more likely to connect Mongol inclinations toward Islam with the religious affiliations of the Turkic populations upon whom the Mongols were always dependent. But Hodgson's attribution of the political stability possible with Islam, particularly with its extension of *dhimmi* status to Christians, Jews, and a few other religions in Central Asia and the Middle East—as well as to Hindus and Buddhists in India—remains persuasive.

In contemporary scholarship on Central Asian history, the general background of military patronage and the household state as Hodgson outlined it is essential to understanding the specifics of cabinet government, by which a ruler depended upon his leading and most-trusted military officers as articulation points between him, the central bureaucracy, and the regional extensions of the bureaucracy. Today this institutional trend is associated with the Mongol *kešig* (*keshig, keshik*), the band of bodyguard and companion dependents who traditionally formed the most-trusted element of the inner state.[9] The institution is now seen as having multiple facets. There is first of all the history of the *kešig* itself in the Mongol empire before 1261, where it is seen specifically as a collection of ostensible bodyguards (a specific sense of the term that continued in the military organization of the Mughals), the elites of whom eventually became the links to provincial military commanders, a source for bureaucratic appointments, and influential advisors at court. Second, the *kešig* is seen as a model of government by a clique of tightly bonded military men that was emulated in many of the Mongol appanages, as well as in Korea. Third, the *kešig* is seen as a matrix out of which new political standards and bureaucratic forms across Eurasia emerged, as this novel nexus of command was superimposed over older and more cumbersome forms of bureaucracy.[10]

Hodgson's views on the relationship between nomadic and sedentary zones owes much to V. V. Bartold and anticipates some of the ideas of Fletcher and those of Thomas Barfield, but his trenchant observations on the historic connections of nomads to urban commercial centers of the desert and the steppe have not been fully incorporated into later scholarship.[11] One reason Hodgson's arguments may not have much reach within modern scholarship runs through volume 3 of the collection, where he asserts that Turks, Mongols, and other nomads were never sources of significant cultural influence over the zones they contacted or even dominated. They wielded influence, when they did, through mechanisms of patronage (sometimes coercive) over artists, artisans, and merchants, which paralleled their patronage of military elites, allowing them to indirectly manipulate social and political evolution in regions where they were an ephemeral presence. This interpretation limits nomads to the role of catalyst in the transition to modernity for Islamic societies. However, recent research on Mongol history by Thomas Allsen,[12] and that by Michal Biran,[13] as well as recent research on Ming, Qing, Russian, and Ottoman history suggest a far more direct effect of nomadic cultural and political influence over the sedentary zones. Vernacular languages, local religious organizations, much smaller governments, lower taxes, higher status for merchants, and a nascent interest in sea power have all been demonstrated to have some degree of direct derivation from persisting nomadic contact—before, during, and after the Mongol empires.[14]

Mongol Influence on Ming Chinese Government

An understanding of the wider influence of the institutions Hodgson linked together as military patronage was undoubtedly hobbled when he dismissed China from his set of Mongol-legacy empires. It is a bit ironic that Hodgson worked in a milieu in which China's tradition of "conquering its conquerors" was still conventional wisdom, yet Hodgson thought that the Mongols were the one thing that China could not absorb. He evidently took seriously the scholarly fashions of the 1950s and 1960s which accepted that the civilian elites of Ming China—including the emperors—were determined to expunge all Mongol elements from their state. After Hodgson's death, scholarship on China clearly delineated a strong Mongol legacy in both the military and the civilian practices of Ming, and of course the Qing had a vivid, direct, overt connection to the Mongol heritage that was the main inspiration for Fletcher's extended comparisons of Ottoman and Qing history as Mongol-legacy states.[15] The discrepancy between Hodgson's assumptions regarding Mongol political legacy outside the Islamic world and the disposition of present scholarship raises the question of how sound Hodgson's assertion was that Islamic states were uniquely receptive to Mongol notions of a small, ruler-centered, military-oriented, but bureaucratically adept elite.

The specifics of Ming retention of Mongol innovations are easily reviewed. They need to be seen as coexisting with a vigorous Ming propaganda rejecting the entire experience of Mongol conquest and occupation and denouncing Mongols everywhere in the strongest terms. Despite this, the Ming retained the radical restructuring of regional administration put in place by the Mongols (the direct source of the modern provincial system in China). The decimal military system introduced by the Mongols was retained across the Ming empire (and would have been used to resist Timur if he had invaded). The academies of astronomy and mathematics established under the Mongols were continued, and for decades Muslims and Mongols were prominent among the staff. The Ming court continued to nurture a special political relationship with Muslim communities, very much in the fashion of the later Mongol rulers in China.[16] A system of social registration that was in essence an elaboration of the system used by the Mongols was instituted. Perhaps one of the most spectacular expressions of Ming continuity of governmental form and representation was the career of the Yongle emperor (1403–24). He moved the capital from Nanjing back to Beijing, sent the Muslim navigator Zheng He (Hajji Mahmud Shams al-Din) on his repeated voyages across the Indian Ocean to the Persian Gulf and the east coast of Africa, and in various other ways announced himself a universal ruler in the style of the Mongol Great Khans.[17]

Assessing the degree to which the Ming state, particularly in the fifteenth century, fulfilled Hodgson's criteria for military patronage has some rewards. In addition to the specific attributes described above, the Ming without doubt displayed evidence of *kešig*-like inner government. The most obvious point of attention is the innovative *neige*, "inner cabinet," a small, trustworthy personal bureaucracy (with the difference that virtually all members were degree holders, though some held the military degree). Through the Ming and Qing periods, as emperors found their inner cabinets to grow in size and become either untrustworthy or unwieldy, they tended to create new inner governments.[18] Members of these inner governments were depended upon to act as envoys or commissioners with special tasks, and some sat at the top of other government departments, keeping the imperial command structure tight and more easily monitored. The style, particularly in the early Ming, far more resembled the Mongol *kešig* than the imperial inner bureaucracies (the *shangshuling*) of the Song period and earlier, even the interlocking *divan* structures of the Ottoman Empire. But more striking was the overall tendency of the Ming to keep the government small and to privatize to the extent possible matters that were not related to the military, census taking, and tax collection.

This does not mean that the Ming government was, beneath a self-conscious Chinese and Confucian veneer, a replication of the Mongol government. The examination system was reinstituted (though based upon an ideological orientation made orthodox under the Mongols); small but important government offices for education and history writing were staffed. Within government and without, civilian dress and standards ostentatiously displaced their military counterparts. Perhaps most important, the frankly expropriative government posture that Hodgson had associated with the military patronage states of western Eurasia was never part of either Ming or Qing presentation. The governments were kept small primarily for the purpose of keeping taxes low and keeping minimal the complications of tax uprisings or other forms of civil resistance, as well as limiting the officials and distances over which the government had to maintain surveillance. Nevertheless, the difference in style may have been little more than that. The early Ming period was one in which the imperial lineage amassed a great deal of wealth, and the Ming Yongle emperor was in the position, as Hodgson remarked respecting ʿAbbas, of "the greatest investor of capital in the realm" (*Venture* 3:55). In fact the Yongle emperor came chronologically between the Ottoman rulers Bayezid and Mehmet II; while their investments went toward the eventual conquest of Constantinople by navies and heavy weapons, the Yongle emperor's investment went toward building the Forbidden City in Beijing and financing the voyages of Zheng He. In the same way that the conquest of Constantinople transformed the Ottoman Empire, the trade impact of the Zheng He voyages might have transformed the Ming—had they not been repudiated as wasteful and too reminiscent of the Mongols by later rulers.

The actual effects of Mongol domination upon China—as well as the particular impact of military patronage upon post-Mongol states across Eurasia—are best seen when simply considering the size of the Ming state. Most historians are now in agreement that in the Song period (970–1279) China was on the cusp of economic, social, and cultural changes which, when they occurred centuries later in other parts of Eurasia, were recognized as "modern." One of these developments was the emergence of a centralized, professional, well-funded bureaucracy supported by an equally professional tax system. Mongol destruction of the Song in 1279 meant, among many other changes, a rapid shrinkage of the size of the state in China. Hodgson's "military patronage" model explains, to a great degree, why. The new state put a premium upon military conquest and occupation, and privatized tax collection, which was often contracted to immigrated Muslim entrepreneurs. The civil functions of the state virtually were frail or nonexistent under the Mongols. The Ming did not return to the Song style of a thick, expensive state. They retained the Mongol model of small government. And the Qing coming after them retained the same model, having a civil government that was virtually the same size as the Ming, despite the fact that Qing administered twice as much territory and three times as much population.

The Mongol Legacy and Eurasian Early Modernity

The tininess of the post-Mongol states in China, organized on principles that strongly echo Hodgson's description of the military patronage states, is illuminated by a comparison to Russia in the early Romanov period. Where the Qing used perhaps 20,000 civilian officials to rule well over 400 million subjects, the tsars used perhaps 10,000 officials to rule perhaps 40 million. The Russian government was thin, the Qing much thinner. Both resemble the tiny governments of the Ottoman Empire and the Mughal government before the coming of the East India Company. The effects of military patronage—or something so like what Hodgson described that we might as well call it military patronage—were evident across Eurasia as huge land empires once organized to support a conquest class and do little else struggled unsuccessfully to meet the onslaught of new military and financial regimes exported by states with comparatively enormous states. By the nineteenth century they contrasted sharply to the emergence of huge states in Britain, Japan, and the United States, capable of launching modernization programs in agriculture, industry, and education.

What is more critical to an understanding of a Eurasian passage of early modernity is the role of governments organized on the Mongol pattern of military patronage in the emergence of centralized, largely secular, states with small governments and thin tax bases. They promoted a certain professionalization of the military and a professional interest in the applied sciences behind engineering, weaponry, and logistics, yet interfered minimally in the commercial development of the agricultural and commercial sectors. This produced courts of the fourteenth through seventeenth centuries that excelled at conquest and grand display (via architecture, artistic patronage, ritual), stimulated the development of many of the fine arts, provoked populations in many areas to begin to think about local identities, self-determination, literacy in vernacular languages, and other concerns that we associate with the transition to modernity. In empires such as the Ottoman, Russian, and Qing, the imperial mandate was explicitly asserted as exceeding the jurisdiction of traditional religious authorities, incorporating a distinctly metacultural and secular element into the rulerships. Nevertheless, these rulerships were transitional. They could not resist the financial, military, or ultimately the aspirational powers of the European sea empires or the late-stage new empires of the United States and Japan. In both time and in space, these empires framed a distinct Eurasian era between the religious domination of the medieval era and the civil societies of the modern period.

Notes

1. "Military patronage" is today a commonly used term but in most cases means the opposite of what Hodgson meant. Today it is used by sociologists and some cultural theorists to mean patronage by the military (or the military establishment, or the "military-industrial complex") of nonmilitary institutions, usually educational and research establishments, but increasingly also producers of popular entertainment, information management, and digital security. Hodgson's meaning was patently a form of traditional patronage of the military populations by the ruler, or militarization of other patronage relationships. Hodgson said in a footnote that the term had been suggested to him in conversation by "Martin Dixon," which I take to be an error—though a very puzzling one—for Martin Dickson. Marshall G. S. Hodgson, *The Venture of Islam: Conscience and History in a World Civilization*, 3 vols. (Chicago: University of Chicago Press, 1974), 3:51 (hereafter cited in the text as *Venture*).

2. For well-known specific applications, see Maria Subtelny's "patrimonial household state," in *Timurids in Transition: Turko-Persian Politics and Acculturation in Medieval Iran*, vol. 7 (Leiden: Brill, 2007), esp. 14–39; and Rhoads Murphey, *Exploring Ottoman Sovereignty: Image and Practice in the Ottoman Imperial Household, 1400–1800* (London: Bloomsbury, 2011), esp. 117–74.

3. Such inscriptions often recursively celebrate an imperial or regional governor's magnificence by reference to the object or building on which the inscription is found; see, among many possibilities, Sheila Blair and Jonathan Bloom, *The Art and Architecture of Islam, 1250–1800* (New Haven, CT: Yale University Press, 1995), 74, 100, 157, 171, 180, 188–89, 208; Catherine Asher, *Architecture of Mughal India*, New Cambridge History of India, vol. 4, pt. 1 (Cambridge: Cambridge University Press, 1992), 78, 93, 102, 109, 120, 157, 236, 311–17.

4. Hodgson clearly accepts the Yasa as a law code—certainly a stable one, and possibly a written one—which is not the current consensus in Mongolian studies. I do however

think that invocation of the Yasa was a mark of elite Mongolian identity both in China and in Iran/Iraq, and so Hodgson's point here might withstand the remarkable changes in the scholarly view since the publication of an essay by David Ayalon in 1971. The historiography, as well as further analysis, is provided in David Morgan, "The 'Great *Yasa* of Chinggis Khan' Revisited," in *Mongols, Turks and Others,* ed. Reuven Amitai and Michal Biran (Leiden: Brill, 2005), 291–308.

5. In Hodgson's view, a pre-Mongol trend in Islamic law interpretation that tended to marginalize the *ʿulamā* and aggrandize the power of the *sultān* also worked to the advantage of Mongol power, even though it was not produced by the Mongols themselves. Hodgson, *Venture,* 2:406.

6. See particularly Joseph F. Fletcher, Jr., and Beatrice Forbe Manzs, eds., *Studies on Chinese and Islamic Inner Asia* (Aldershot, UK: Variorum, 1995); and Fletcher, "Turco-Mongolian Monarchical Tradition in the Ottoman Empire," *Harvard Ukrainian Studies* 3/4 (1979–1980): 236–51.

7. See Michael Cherniavsky, "Khan or Basileus: An Aspect of Russian Mediaeval Political Theory," *Journal of the History of Ideas* 20, no. 4 (October–December 1959): 459–76; and Cherniavsky, *Tsar and People: Studies in Russian Myths* (New Haven, CT: Yale University Press, 1961).

8. I do think "tolerance" (which in reference to the Mongols is conventionally traced to Gibbon) is a suitable word for describing the attitudes of some Mongol rulers and aristocrats toward religious affiliation. Peter Jackson, "The Mongols and the Faith of the Conquered," in *Mongols, Turks and Others,* ed. Reuven Amitai and Michal Biran (Leiden: Brill, 2005), 245–91, reviews the origins of the impression of religious "tolerance" among the Mongols, see esp. 253–59. I agree with Devin Deweese that it is unwise to allow oneself unbridled attribution of what is a distinctly modern ethos (even if that ethos itself is misnamed in this case) to the Mongol regimes. See also Devin Deweese, *Islamization and Native Religion in the Golden Horde: Baba Tükles and Conversion to Islam in Historical and Epic Tradition* (State College: Pennsylvania State University Press, 1994), esp. 90–102. Earlier, Anatoly Khazanov had already usefully contrasted tolerance and accommodation ("Muhammad and Jenghiz Khan Compared: The Religious Factor in World Empire Building," *Comparative Studies in Society and History* 35, no. 3 [July 1993]: 461–79), and Halperin had perhaps even more usefully characterized pre-Islamic Mongol policy on religion as not tolerance but indifference ("The Ideology of Silence: Prejudice and Pragmatism on the Medieval Religious Frontier," *Comparative Studies in Society and History* 26, no. 3 [July 1984]: 442–66). Christopher P. Atwood, "Validation by Holiness or Sovereignty: Religious Toleration as Political Theology in the Mongol World Empire of the Thirteenth Century," *International History Review* 26, no. 2 (June 2004): 236–56, ascribes to the pre-Islamic Mongol regimes a "political theology" that permitted tax privileges to patronized religions whose ideas of supernatural affirmation of Mongol rule could be utilized, and suppression of religions or sects that were incompatible (or otherwise a distinct threat, as in the case of the Ismailis).

9. See, for instance, David Robinson, *Empire's Twilight: Northeast Asia under the Mongols* (Cambridge, MA: Harvard University Press, 2009); Christopher Beckwith, *Empires of the Silk Road: A History of Central Eurasia from the Bronze Age to the Present* (Princeton, NJ: Princeton University Press, 2009), 19–22.

10. On the transition of the *kešig* from soldiers to governmental factotums, see particularly Thomas T. Allsen, "Guard and Government in the Reign of the Grand Qan Möngke," *Harvard Journal of Asiatic Studies* 27, no. 2 (1986): 495–521; Charles Melville, "The *Keshig* in Iran: The Survival of the Royal Mongol Household," in *Beyond the Legacy of Genghis Khan*, ed. Linda Komaroff (Leiden: Brill, 2006) 41–45; Subtelny, *Timurids in Transition*, 18–23; Ch'i Ch'ing Hsiao, *The Military Establishment of the Yuan Dynasty* (Cambridge, MA: Harvard University Press, 1978). In Tibet *kashag* became the term for a governing council (imposed by the Qing in the eighteenth century) and is today the term for the cabinet leading the exile government in Dharamsala.

11. See important commentary here of Beatrice Forbes Manz, *Power, Politics and Religion in Timurid Iran* (Cambridge: Cambridge University Press, 2007), 117–18, 316–17.

12. Particularly Thomas T. Allsen, *Mongol Imperialism: The Policies of the Grand Qan Möngke in China, Russia, and the Islamic Lands, 1251–1259* (Berkeley: University of California Press, 1987); Allsen, *Commodity and Exchange in the Mongol Empire: A Cultural History of Islamic Textiles* (Cambridge: Cambridge University Press, 1997); Allsen, *Culture and Conquest in Mongol Eurasia* (Cambridge: Cambridge University Press, 2001).

13. Michal Biran, *Qaidu and the Rise of the Independent Mongol State in Central Asia* (Richmond, Surrey, UK: Curzon Press, 1997); Reuven Amitai and Michal Biran, eds., *Mongols, Turks and Others: Eurasian Nomads and the Sedentary World* (Leiden: Brill, 2005); *Chinggis Khan* (Oxford: Oneworld, 2007).

14. For extended discussion see my forthcoming book, *Nomad Rulers and the Threshold of the Modern World* (Lanham, MD: Rowman & Littlefield).

15. This subject is treated at length in my book *A Translucent Mirror: History and Identity in Qing Imperial Ideology* (Berkeley: University of California Press, 1999).

16. See Zvi Ben-Dor Benite, *The Dao of Muhammad: A Cultural History of Muslims in Later Imperial China* (Cambridge, MA: Harvard East Asian Monographs, 2005).

17. For more background, see Morris Rossabi, "The Ming and Inner Asia," in *The Cambridge History of China*, vol. 8, *The Ming Dynasty, 1368–1644* (Cambridge: Cambridge University Press, 1998); and Rossabi, "Notes on Mongol Influences in the Ming Dynasty," in *Eurasian Influences on Yuan China*, ed. Rossabi (Singapore: Institute of Southeast Asian Studies, 2013), 200–223.

18. For a close study of this in the Qing, see Beatrice S. Bartlett, *Monarchs and Ministers: The Grand Council in Mid-Ch'ing China, 1723–1820* (Berkeley: University of California Press, 1994).

Hodgson and the New Islamic Studies

CHAPTER EIGHT

Harems and Cathedrals

THE QUESTION OF GENDER AND SEXUALITY IN THE WORK OF MARSHALL HODGSON

Jocelyne Dakhlia

TRANSLATED BY EDMUND BURKE III

While today we are discovering the impact of Marshall Hodgson on world history, there's little sense in not making him also a precursor of another history, one that is crucial at the present time: that of gender. To be sure, questions of gender and sexuality were not in the front of his mind. However, thoughts about the frontiers of gender are not only a present and recurrent theme in Hodgson's work overall, but Hodgson's profoundly egalitarian reading of Islam raises the question, itself complex, of the relations of the sexes. His problematic, more than that of others, leads him to a comparative approach with all that it implies about systemization and about frontiers.[1]

Many of Hodgson's most important observations on gender and sexuality in Islamic societies can be found in volume 2 of *The Venture of Islam*, notably in "Cultural Patterning in Islamdom and the Occident."[2] They are also discussed in several other chapters in *Venture*, especially "Family Law: Pressure toward Equality in Personal Status" (1:340–44). More importantly, in the second volume he analyzes at length not only the question of the relations of gender, as well as questions relative to the family, relations of kinship, but also the question of sexuality itself, which he approaches with a sometimes surprising realism.

The chronological context that he privileges in this approach (as has often been emphasized) is that of the full expansion of Islamic culture in what he calls the "Middle Periods," basically the twelfth and thirteenth centuries, following the fall of the absolutist caliphates and the onset of a phase of political fragmentation dominated by the *amir-aʿyan* system. This section is more focused within the frame of the "structure" in a kind of historical anthropology, rather than on the history properly speaking. For Hodgson, the Middle Periods were marked by the completion of the blueprint of Islamic society at its most logical, as well as of the "Irano-Mediterranean" Islamic world. The issues of the definition of the family and of the place of women, or even the ways of being man or woman, lead him to juxtapose the Islamic model and other models, notably a Western or European, or even Christian, model.

These questions hold our attention and invite us to a more fine-grained reading, because of what they reveal about the oscillations of Hodgson's thought between a systematic, structural way of thinking, like that of an ideal type, and a profoundly historical way of thinking, one more fully integrated into history. We must never forget that while he was always thinking about questions of gender, Hodgson's thought is complex, dense, and difficult, if also always fully inscribed in the history of its time.[3] If most current studies of gender in Islamic societies can today find numerous points of filiation and convergence in the writings of Marshall Hodgson, this is no reason not to view his brilliant work as being completely original.

Segments and Arabesques

The extreme power of Marshall Hodgson's thought lies in its deconstruction of any a priori opposition between Islamic history and European history. In a powerful footnote (*Venture* 1:281n1), he devotes himself to sweeping away the idea of oriental despotism, then maintained with conviction by Karl Wittfogel. While his analyses, in both large and small strokes, work to empty of meaning both cultural preconceptions and frontiers,[4] nonetheless questions of gender seem, on the contrary, to both attract and repel him. The pages that Hodgson devotes to this subject refer certainly to what he called the Irano-Mediterranean cultural zone, including at times the European Mediterranean, but the core of his argument resides more often on a strongly antithetical vision, that opposes systematically a European social system and an Islamic social system. Structure clearly defeats history in this demonstration.

The demonstration is magnificent both in its unbelievable coherence and logic. Hodgson opposes term by term a Western society marked by legitimacy and hierarchy to an Islamic society marked by the opposite—contractualism and egalitarianism. A strongly corporatist society of recognized groups and privileges versus a society of individuals and personal merit.[5] For Hodgson the Gothic cathedral and Gothic art symbolize the Western affinity for hierarchy, elevation, and centrality. In it one sees in a metonymic manner the attachment to finished, completed constructions and to statuses limited to the meanings from which they derive and based upon the organic connection to a group: "Rigid autonomous units, organized according to mutual hierarchical relations in the context of a closed and rigidly structured whole."[6]

Nevertheless on a concrete, architectural basis, the Gothic arch has its equivalent in Islamic structures, this common architectural language containing rather different meanings in the two cases. The cathedral and the mosque do not use the arch and the ogive in the same manner, Islam conferring upon them an entirely new meaning.[7] For Hodgson these differences operate on a symbolic level in which the cathedral symbolizes the Occident, and the arabesque the Islamic world. Certainly, Hodgson would concede that the Islamic world has no architectural equivalent to the cathedral, but for him just as the arabesque crystallizes an aesthetic form, so too it crystallizes Islam's social "style." He sees in the unfinished reproduction of the latter, in its possibly infinite repetition, the mark of a form of egalitarianism inherent in Islamic culture and in Islamic societies. This structuring principle of equality expresses itself in the repetition of the same motifs, or even similar motifs superposed upon one another: "To put the overall style in a formula corresponding to what we used for the Occident, the sense of good order demanded a pattern *of equal and transferable units satisfying a single set of fixed standards in a field penetrable to several levels and universally extendable.*"[8] Hodgson links the verticality of the cathedral and the finiteness of its proportions to the corporatism and basic legitimacy of forms of Western social organization, as well as to some intellectual productions: demonstrative geometry, the art of the syllogism, etcetera.[9]

He symmetrically opposes the aesthetic of the arabesque with that of the *isnad* of prophetic tradition and that of the Sufi *silsila* notably as interpersonal chains, with the idea of a self-activated proliferation, so to speak.[10] Jacques Berque, whose thought resembles that of Hodgson in certain respects, also employed an approach that consisted in using an aesthetic motif to refer to a cultural essence. Berque identified the "star polygon" as a cultural motif of the Islamic world, an emblematic and extensive motif of Islamic cultural coherence, one that is infinitely reproducible.[11] (Berque included in his reading a sexual and erotic dimension, since he saw in the points of the polygon star the aesthetic of a "male emptiness," a conquering "push. . . .")[12] In Hodgson's perspective the motif of the arabesque is also a principle of order. For example, in the transmission of historical tales: "the equally expandable corpus of historical tales, each documented and certified on a level of equality with all the rest, allows the seemingly chaotic variety of life's reality to be reduced to manageable order, without arbitrarily setting bounds to it either in extent or in depth of meaning."[13]

A principle of equality of segments (composing the arabesque, or the social institutions) is inherent in his reading of Islamic societies, as an echo of his attraction for the historical period in the course of which caliphal power waned before small political structures, *aʿyan* and *amirs*, in the form of a negation or salutary eclipse of the State. This equality surely echoes his own religious convictions and the principle of equality between "brothers" or "sisters," but its formulations can also be seen in the famous principle of Kharijism, according to which the imamate should go to whichever male was the most worthy, "even a black slave." "These personal responsibilities of office in Islam were conceived on an egalitarian basis: in principle, they might be assumed by anyone who was qualified, once he became a Muslim, whatever his antecedents."[14]

The power of the *amir*, of course, is a power of the moment, negotiated and not inscribed in the social tissue of the lineage. It is based upon what Hodgson calls in heuristic fashion Islamic "occasionalism" and it is accompanied in a structural manner by a form of violence and arbitrariness (*Venture* 2:343). Indeed, this power is not inherited, nor is it the fruit of the legitimacy of a social body; its power derives from the personal value and from a moment, in which arbitrariness is always possible to bring "peers" to reason. Hodgson here seeks to contrast the limits of the occidental system, where the principle of heredity can lead to aberrations (for example, the accession of a weak or mental incompetent to the throne), with that of the Islamic system, which can upon occasion give free rein to arbitrary violence (2:346).

In deploying this demonstration, Hodgson underscores the radical contrast between Western (or even "Hindu") societies that recognize primogeniture due to their legitimist essence and Islamic societies, which do not recognize it, in the name of a principle of equality applying to all the sons. Transposed in the case of princely or ruling families, this rule explains the relatively peaceful dynastic transitions in Europe, as well as the conflicted and troubled interregnums in Islam, where each pretender to the throne must prove his personal valor, the orderliness of succession not being the rule. It is true that in places the principle of inherited status seem to be the prerogative, and he notably extends this observation (central to his egalitarian demonstration) to the Zoroastrians, but always in opposition to the Islamic world.

The Islamic logic of the "segment," the term Hodgson preferred to the term "motif," no doubt evokes the term "segmentarity," in vogue in anthropological theory at just this time with reference to Islamic societies from Afghanistan to Morocco, including the Sudan.[15] Anthropology in the school of Evans-Pritchard rather than that of Durkheim sought to explain social and political order in societies lacking a strong state, or in the total absence of a state. Here we can see at work the same fascination with a politically egalitarian and stateless order. However, segmentary anthropology never attempted to explain as well and to the same degree the social logics, including the basis of the family and gender relations.

Hodgson, with a brilliance that sometimes led him to exaggerate, extended the system of opposition between the Occident and Islam into the domestic sphere, up to and including conjugal and family relations. He saw social roles in Islamic societies as being regulated by contract, rather than deriving from heritage. Marriage in Islamic societies he insists, was a disputable and reversible contract, and not a sacrament.[16] (Similarly, "contractualism" in the social sphere when transposed into the visual field became the arabesque.)[17] As for the role of the spouses, it involves also a contractual engagement among other contractual egalitarian responsibilities: "This means that legitimate authority is attributed to its actions which derive from personal responsibilities assumed in the roles such as emir in a city, the imam in prayer, the ghazi [fighting] on the frontier, the husband in a family."[18]

The antithetical demonstration established in his structural opposition of the Occident and Islam logically governs and concerns the most intimate order of the family, the household:

> Among the Christians and Mazdeans (as in most societies), such wealthy men as maintained more than one woman had to accord special privileges to a primary mate and her children. Among the Mazdeans the secondary mates received some legal protection and their children might under some circumstances inherit. Among the Christians, the secondary mates had in principle no rights whatever and their children were stigmatized as mere bastards (though in practice such "natural sons," in contrast to the offspring of casual unions, sometimes might maintain a high position, just as in the Medieval Occident the bar sinister sometimes inherited not only good breeding and wealth, but even lands and sometimes titles). (*Venture* 1:340–41)

(Sometimes he frames it as a distinction between Islam and other societies, including Zoroastrians.)

Further, Hodgson views the Western world as regulated by an active hierarchical principle found in the bosom of the family (and thus inscribing the vertical and hierarchical model of the cathedral). From this perspective, the spouse as sole mistress of the house is a partner assured of her position and status, from which her husband cannot divorce her. She reigns over a domestic world, itself hierarchically organized with its domestic servants of inferior rank. If her husband has other sexual partners (a frequent tendency of well-born men, according to Hodgson), they can occupy only a second-rank position, or even that of a prostitute. Their children, too, are divided between legitimate and illegitimate.[19]

By contrast, he views the Muslim household as governed by the strict principle of equality: equality between free spouses, protected by the same laws, and equality of their children no matter who their mothers might be, who also enjoy equal rights regardless of their place in the birth order: "The Sharîʿah looked to the opposite extreme from this, placing all the man's free sexual partners on the same level, as well as their children, and governing their position by contract, giving none of them an indefeasible status such as an undivorceable materfamilias could have."[20] Although the question is scarcely developed in his analyses, he defines the *umm walad*, the slave mother, freed and endowed with inalienable rights as a free sexual partner.

On the case of the plurality of wives, Hodgson provides a modern and incisive vision, in an analysis of great acuity inserted (as he often does) in a simple but powerful footnote. At this point in the analysis he declines (to assert) an illusory opposition not only between Western monogamy and Islamic polygyny, but also between the West and the rest of the world, where he reminds us polygyny is dominant: "In older writings, 'monogamy' and 'polygamy' were usually distinguished as the two contrasting normal forms of marriage—Christians practicing the one and most other peoples the other. (As 'monogamy' had prestige value, too often writers intending to justify various non-Christian social systems tried to show they were in fact monogamous, sometimes even by taking note that polygamy was practiced 'only by a minority'—overlooking the fact that this is no special merit, or it is usually guaranteed by the laws of nature.)" It appears to him, contrary to what is commonly believed, that the opposition between polygamy and monogamy does not adequately capture the contrast between the Occident and the Islamic world: "This conventional dichotomy unfortunately obscures artificially many of the most important questions. Not only does it make too sharp a distinction between systems that differ much less in practice (because of the custom of keeping mistresses). It hides the points of real difference. Thus the presence of a slave-based 'harem' system, even with only one wife, may be socially more decisive than the presence of two unsecluded wives."[21]

First and foremost, Hodgson relativizes the supposed monogamy of Western societies, in recalling the often highly institutionalized existence of mistresses, especially among men of high status: "And where there are secondary partners, their status may determine family patterns as decisively as that of the primary partner, who alone tends to be taken into account in discussing 'monogamy'" (*Venture* 1:341).

In volume 3 of *Venture* Hodgson reminds us that the Bible justifies polygyny at least as much as the Quran, and that some Christian churches moreover practiced it (3:408). But he equally and systematically sweeps away the argument of the defenders of Islam that believe it good to recall that Muslim societies were de facto monogamous, since only a small minority of men had multiple wives (1:340n12). According to him, the chief contrast doesn't reside in the principle of monogyny or plural marriage, but in the status of secondary sexual partners and the rights accorded to their children. Now Islamic polygyny, from his perspective, is conceived in the form of an extension of the reproduction of segments. Hodgson reminds us himself of the small proportion of polygynist unions (well known in historical demography and generally never more than 5 percent of couples): "everywhere rare save among the wealthy" (1:181n25). The nuclear family—father, mother, children—is simply plural in an intersection of nuclear cells and under the authority of a sole master of the house.[22] Although in the Occident family rights are, with a few exceptions, reserved to the sole legitimate wife and to her children as a principle of legitimacy, of corporatism and hierarchy symbolized by the cathedral, the Muslim sharia oversees that the rights are equally shared by all of the children.

Thus when a son in an Islamic city took up the professional occupation of his father, this was not a sign of corporatism but the result of a form of individual freedom and a sign of personal merit. The multiplicity of sexual partners of a father, in higher social classes, in giving birth to sons of equal status would multiply the chances that he would find among them an individual capable of maintaining the family tradition. Certainly, girls inherited a smaller share than their brothers, but all children inherited and had rights to assert. Even the children of slaves and concubines of low status and those not of a legal wife were equal among themselves in legal terms. It is here that Hodgson must conceive of and recognize in spite of everything a bending of the rules of egalitarianism of the sharia in the domestic sphere. The point on which the sharia permitted the perpetuation of a flagrant inequality is the question of slavery (*Venture* 1:182).

Egalitarianism and Its Limits

For Hodgson everything is logically interconnected. While the Prophet Muhammad would not have encouraged sexual relations with other partners than legally married wives, these practices were thrust aside in upper social classes, for a reason that Hodgson connects with the diffusion of the *amir-a'yan* system (*Venture* 1:182). If the local notables (the *a'yan*) agreed to confer political power to military rulers (the *amirs*) foreign to the local society, it was in everyone's interest to avoid matrimonial alliances that might go against this arrangement and its logic by multiplying the kinship pressures upon politics and the public sphere. In other words, Hodgson here identifies the logic that will be otherwise described in the case of the Mamluk system and the Ottoman administrative model.[23] The recourse to slave women is the means of preserving a form of restriction in the family reproduction and in the management of the social and political order. But slavery in itself provides a kind of logical and moral scandal for Hodgson, as a Quaker and as a moral man, and if he recognizes the logical rationalities (commerce and mobility inherent in the entire social system, carrying men to the frontiers of the Islamic ecumene, and leading them also to bring back slaves), he despairs of it and attempts to modulate this inequality: "We may suggest that slavery by import (as against a more home-bred peasant serfdom) was retained in Islamdom partly because of the relative access of the wealthy Muslim cities to frontier areas of the Oikoumene where captives were available; but primarily because an egalitarian and socially mobile society seemed to require, in an agrarian age, such a class to set off those who momentarily had risen to the top."[24]

Thus in the occidental world as in the Islamic world a woman manages the house of her spouse, but by virtue of a statute of hierarchical dominion, in the first instance, reflecting the vertical model of the cathedral. In the second instance, the Islamic one, she cohabits with secondary sexual partners of low status, who nonetheless are perfectly integrated into the space of the house, where they are recognized as having a place and official rights. The repetitive logic of the harem is perfectly congruent with the principle of the arabesque.

Another consequence derives from this. While the masculine society is regulated, as has been underscored, by a principle of great social mixing, where the status of an individual is personal and is defined in the light of his proper merit, the segregation of women, excluded from the public space, appears as the means of preserving this social mingling. Of course it is this social ensemble, harem included, that is structured in its cosmopolitanism and its social mixing:

> The *a'yân-amîr* system and, more generally, the cosmopolitan tendencies of the mid-Arid Zone were reflected indirectly in the private life of the more privileged classes, which in turn helped to undergird the distinctive traits of public life. The slave household (or "harem system") characteristic of upper-class Islamdom presupposed the social mobility of the society, the mingling of classes and the open and shifting lines of patronage among the *a'yân* notables. In contrast to upper-class households in the Occident or in Hindu India guaranteed by fixed social status, the Muslim household might preserve a reasonably fixed character only by way of slavery and female seclusion. (*Venture* 2:140)

One might underline in passing the concept of "acculturation" in these analyses, an anthropologically based concept then well represented in the social sciences, which conceived of culture as diffusing from higher classes to lower classes.[25] The acculturation was, however, a crucial notion in the midst of the 1970s discussion of the "new history." (We can note the distance between this linear reading and the nonreciprocal readings that have emerged over the last several decades.) The perspective of acculturation as a form of cultural homogenization lies within the logic of Hodgson's egalitarian demonstration, or rather in the logic of a society seen as an ensemble of similar and equal entities. Anyway, in a competition between women with equal rights the only way for a woman to claim social distinction was to accept her own seclusion and, naturally to veil herself:

> The mingling of all classes among the males, encouraged by Muslim disregard of inherited rank, threw all levels together on intimate terms; if men and women had mingled freely, this could have tended to eliminate any remaining aura of respect for well-born wives. If the women might have been content to take the consequences of a free and relatively contractual position, the men were not willing to have it so. It early became a mark of a woman of quality that she was secluded from all men but her own—in private apartments at home, behind a veil if she walked abroad. (*Venture* 1:341)

It follows for Hodgson that the veil is found in urban societies, in a descending manner, from the higher classes to the middle classes such that in the bottom end only lower-class women working in public space remain outside this system of social distinction of the veil and female seclusion.

Hodgson saw how this system fostered social distinction extremely well—a topic today so absent in civic debates about the veil and Islam. In support of this social dynamic, Hodgson emphasizes that this is anchored in a historical tendency to imitate the wives of the Prophet, showing that there were originally no restrictions on women's behavior other than modesty and respect for family privacy (*Venture* 1:343). Subsequently, he describes clearly the mimetic logic of the ruling classes, by which the veil and female segregation practices spread, even though they were not promoted by the sharia. The number of wives allowed a simple believer (four legal wives) could not equal the Quranic exception recognized for the Prophet (1:342–43).

The physical separation of men and women needed to be thought (through) as such. True to his approach, Hodgson begins by recontextualizing the subject beyond its cultural or historical specificity. Without calling it a *gyneceum*, he draws parallels with Byzantium and ancient Greece (2:143). The seclusion of women was also practiced, he reminds us, in Byzantium and Persia (1:342). Nonetheless, he admits that segregation by gender had advanced further in the Irano-Mediterranean world than elsewhere. Why? It is at this point in the argument that we must invoke his definition of honor.

The idea of honor occupies a central place in his argument and even provides the title of a subsection: "Sex, Slavery and the Harem System: The Cult of Masculine Honor" (2:301). How is it that Hodgson, who had resolutely separated the Arab world as the epicenter of the Islamic world returns here to so Mediterrano-centric a vision as is implied by the problematic of honor in these years? The scientific moment that is his is that which is filled with the Mediterranean theme of honor, and Hodgson refers in a note to the work edited in this context by John Peristiany with the comment: "He speaks of the Mediterranean but of course these points apply to the entire Irano-Mediterranean complex" (2:142n20).[26]

This Mediterranean, if not Mediterraneanist, perspective is in fact not absent. The author of *The Venture of Islam* hereby evokes the way in which southern Europe, Sicily for example, participates in these practices of jealousy with regard to women and their segregation, and he conceives of honor in terms of popular cultures, "the Iran-Mediterranean folk-cultural homogeneity" (2:140). However this Mediterranean base remains relative:

> Especially in Mediterranean Europe, where women tended to be secluded and domineered in both communities, the Christian marital pattern and the Muslim could look very much alike in the ordinary case; yet in special

> cases the two legal constructions had sufficiently different consequences to set, cumulatively, a different tone. The Christian system sanctified—and under favorable circumstances surely fostered—a solidarity of interest in a couple committed to a single marital union despite the temptations of wealth. The Muslim system sacrificed the primacy of conjugal unity in favor of equality of rights on the part of all concerned. (1:341)

As for the strict question of honor, he agrees that its character is culturally noncircumscribed: "One must first describe these expressions of masculine honor in terms that may be applicable to many peoples, not only those who became Muslim; then, however, one can distinguish the points were the special conditions of Islamdom and especially of the Middle Periods seem to have evoked special effects—which in turn affected the Islamicate high-cultural life" (2:140). Far from him therefore is any narrow vision of a Mediterranean cultural hearth (even his reference to the ethnologist Germaine Tillion and her well-known book *The Harem and Its Cousins* remains critical).[27] It is nonetheless true that he adheres to the conventional idea of a particular exacerbation of this sensibility in the Islamic world (including crimes of honor). The difference from other readings is that in his version, the meaning of honor does not denote a cultural essentialism. On the contrary, it proceeds from a social dynamic inherent in all of the founding principles of the social order.

For Hodgson the sense of honor in these contexts does not reside in an offense against the status of a man, which, he suggests, is offended in his statutory legitimacy as it is conceived in India or northern Europe (*Venture* 2:141). In the Irano-Mediterranean zone, on the contrary, honor always concerns in the first place the personal *worth* of a man. If a family or a neighborhood (*quartier*) together defends the honor of one of its members, it acts according to the same logic, to reply to a personal offense. One might find this reading to be perfectly unrealistic and false, but the point of interest to us here is the manner in which Hodgson interprets the sexual jealousy of men, and thus the practices of the segregation of women, as a logical counterpart to a system of social egalitarianism in which men of various social statuses and origins mix together and, on the basis of personal aptitudes, rival one another in the social space. The more men define themselves in a precarious manner by their personal worth, without inherited and fixed standing, the more they invest in their honor as men, the more they invest in "pure masculinity," or what he calls "*sheer masculinity*" (2:140).

Relations to women become the place where this gender-mixed situation is suspended, and, must one add, this competition. However, historically sexual segregation, once past the foundational period of Islam, was gradually accompanied by a confinement not only of wives (which was conceivable in the original sharia) but also of other women, dependents, slaves, servants over whom their spouses exercised authority, instituting the "harem system" (which in contrast could not be entirely approved by the sharia).[28]

What about the relations of men to one another? For Hodgson, there is one institution that illustrates masculine egalitarianism par excellence: *futuwwah* men's clubs (*Venture* 2:125ff.). The *futuwwah,* he explains, were brotherhoods whose increasingly popular character and social collaborative aspects sometimes spilled over into banditry (2:128). Just as "the harem system" made women of different origins live together, the *futuwwah* system brought together men of different geographic and social origins. It constituted a receiving structure that welcomed strangers and also integrated slaves (like the institution of the harem, as we have seen). Better yet, and this point is crucial with respect to models of masculinity, Hodgson notes that the *futuwwah* brotherhoods even received eunuchs: "The futuwwah naturally tended to supplement an interest in sports with a degree of military discipline; and such a discipline was normally directed at least potentially against the established powers. Commonly *futuwwah* clubs might admit non-Muslim *dhimmis;* they might admit slaves and even eunuchs; but not a coward nor a tax-collector nor the henchman of a tyrant; that is, of an *amîr*" (2:128).

Contrary to a modern historiography that tends to view the eunuch as a kind of intermediary sexual category between men and women, Hodgson, in a simple note, restores to eunuchs their (just) assignment to the masculine gender.[29] The question of civic and political participation as seen in the case of the eunuchs resembles the inscription of gender. Further, Hodgson distinguishes a structural opposition between masculine and feminine as Pierre Bourdieu systematized it in this moment and in a context of strong structuralism.[30] In a single phrase he succeeds, on the contrary, in inscribing a plurality of masculine models, a plurality based upon social class: "The image of the ideal man might vary from class to class" (*Venture* 2:140). In an even more lucid and incisive manner he insists in a note on the fact that there was no necessary equivalence between practices of effeminacy and homosexual practices:[31]

> Unexamined sexual assumptions have entered—usually rather inexplicitly—into Occidental impressions of Muslim mores so frequently that it is necessary to be as clear as possible as to just what is being referred to in the oblique remarks Western literature is full of. Perhaps it is becoming less

> necessary nowadays to point out that an inclination to have sex with other men—even when such sex is actually preferred to sex with women—need not imply effeminacy in any degree (though in some spectacular cases, especially with transvestites, it does so). It must still be pointed out, in some circles, that public display of affection between men, as by walking hand in hand, need not imply any sexual interest. (*Venture* 2:146)

To stay with this last point, sometimes formulated as "homosensuality," one can note, with a bit of distance and humor, that it is at the end under the sign of such a homo-proximity that Hisham Sharabi, in his memoirs, evokes his own friendship with Hodgson. He affirms that having lived for thirty years in the United States, he had been unable to develop any friendship with a man because the conception of masculine friendship wasn't the same as in his own society. Sharabi declares that he preferred the company of American women, not for sexual or emotional reasons, he explains, but because he shared with them more satisfactions and pleasures. Marshall Hodgson would seem an exception to this rule. Sharabi evokes their friendly meetings, swimming pool conversations, and shared sandwiches on the steps of the Library of Congress.[32]

As much as Hodgson displayed an aptitude to understand the segregation of the sexes without overinterpretation, to what extent did he analyze the feminine and masculine universes as distinct? Or, to formulate the question in a perspective closer to his egalitarian views (or the egalitarianism he imputes to the Muslim sharia) what place remains in this social device for the equality he imputes to the Muslim sharia? The household is placed under the authority of a man (even if the power reality, he suggests several times, is often held by women: "In each of the two societies, the husband and father of the family was a dominant and even despotic figure who had final power of decision; in each of the two societies, the wife in fact often ruled the husband").[33]

The authority is formally masculine; it belongs to the father of the family to watch over not only the women of his house (a category extending far beyond wives) but to support their needs and those of their children. According to Hodgson, this domestic model was imposed on those commonly prevalent in the pre-Islamic world (by preventing the enlarged families from interfering in the marriage relationship in particular) (*Venture* 1:181). The counterpart of masculine authority was a series of protections guaranteed to women and their children by the sharia but the family right protected also and especially the members of the household against any despotism or excess of power by the paterfamilias. And in mentioning despotism in the primary sense of the paterfamilias we rediscover a form of metonymy of caliphal absolutism, of absolute power in relation to which Hodgson reacted as a defender of the rights of the individual against the power of the state and absolutist governments: "In discussing family law, it is convenient to consider the rights of women, children, and other dependents as against the male head of the family, who by nature, if law makes no contrary provision, is in the most advantaged position being not only, on the average, stronger than a woman but more independent, since he is free of pregnancy and the immediate care of children. Family law largely consists of restrictions upon his presumed freedom." Such at least is the original spirit of Muslim law though Hodgson insistently underlines that it was not maintained with the same requirement as in later periods of Islamic history (*Venture* 1:340).

It is thus because even a gender hierarchy rooted in the supposed "nature" of women being less physically fit that Hodgson sees at work in egalitarian tension a legal device tending to offset and to reduce inequality. The inferiority of the social condition of women therefore does not proceed from Islamic law, in his eyes. So much so that he emphasizes the unrecognized a priori rights of women, for which there is little evidence based upon the observations of individuals from outside the Islamic world. In a very concrete manner, conjugal sexuality for example is for them an explicit right, and Hodgson does not hesitate to mention a very realistic anecdote about a saint from Shiraz, a tale illustrating the rights of women to assured regular conjugal relations. In the tale it is about a person whose wives all thought he preferred someone else. He finished by showing them that by abstinence, by renouncing sexuality and the pleasures of the world: "till one of them boldly asked him about it and he showed her the knotted flesh of his belly, which he said was the result of restraining himself from eating and from having sex" (*Venture* 2:142). The final commentary that Hodgson provides about this hagiographic account would not be out of place were it written by a contemporary feminist: "The (male) narrator tells the story as an exemplary case of self-denial, and shows no awareness that from a feminine viewpoint it might equally illustrate selfish cruelty" (2:142–43).

For all of that, the masculine and feminine fields of action are not completely different. Hodgson brings to bear an accent completely devoid of anecdotic value in the first place, on episodes of feminine command, starting at the beginning of the thirteenth century with Raziyyah, daughter of Iltumish, who was selected by her father, the sultan of Delhi, to succeed him (*Venture* 2:278).[34] While an abundant twentieth-century literature inquires into the exclusion of Muslim women from political authority, targeting with fascination a few exceptions to the rule, Hodgson refers to a few of these historical episodes from the "Middle Periods" as evidence of assumed equalitarianism, citing also the case of a Mamluk sultana (2:278). To his way of thinking, the exclusion of women from command functions derives not by virtue of their feminine *nature* or of a gender differential, but because of their lesser physical force—an essential question, today in the contemporary scientific debate where this is seen as a difference constitutive of the sexes and not a continuum—the old tradition of seeing in women a less-functioning but similar version of a man. "It was rare (although not unknown) for a child, a woman, or a physically incapacitated man to be accepted for long unless he had a powerful protector; for, as the political ruler was essentially an amir, a military commander, a woman was disqualified insofar as she was not qualified to be a soldier at all." Such at least is the original spirit of Muslim law which Hodgson insistently underlines that it was not maintained with the same requirement as in later periods of Islamic history.[35]

In second place, in a less original way Marshall Hodgson refers to the egalitarian place occupied by women in the mystical tradition and in teaching (*Venture* 1:343). He then reminds us that the famous thirteenth-century theologian Ibn Taymiyyah had studied under the direction of a woman: "Yet even in the Later Middle Periods, when the earlier Muslim tolerance of public roles had long since receded, women could be prominent teachers of the religious disciplines. The zealous legist Ibn-Taymiyyah, among others, had studied under a woman at Damascus" (2:242). The case of Aisha, the preferred wife of the Prophet, allows him to remind us that women had been recognized as traditionalists (*muhaddith*). But the principle of equality seems to have declined with the social and mimetic increase over the centuries of female segregation—an evolution he insists that had not been foreseen: "The debilitation of upper-class women which followed upon rigorous segregation was unforeseen" (1:343).

Does that make Hodgson an Islamic feminist? There were many masculine claimants to this status in the Islamic world in the nineteenth century. Hodgson was well aware of them, referring notably to Qasim Amin, a nineteenth-century pioneer in this matter (3:288–89). But if Hodgson was a feminist in some ways, it was not according to a principle founded upon the single question of women, but rather a logical deduction, a general egalitarian imperative deriving from the entirety of his definition of the sharia. What is certain is that Hodgson's account of the early days of Islam, or rather his idealist reading of sharia law with respect to women's emancipation logically endorses the approach of the first Muslim feminism (or rather the first Muslim feminisms). By the turn of the nineteenth century, feminist positions (emanating from men and women) were never disconnected from encompassing political and social issues where the woman question acted as a lever.[36] The feminist rehabilitation of original Islam is one of the principal components of these currents or of some of them, including their recent extensions. Fatima Mernissi, one of the best-known Arab women intellectuals, precociously exposed historical doubts about the misogynic transmission of Muslim traditions, calling for their critical reinterpretation.[37] We know that this is particularly the task on which different currents of "Muslim feminism" work, alongside other religious feminisms.

Thus Hodgson evoked explicitly a historical form of decline in the status of women tied to social evolution, and not to religious texts, properly speaking (*Venture* 2:417). At the present time some figures of Muslim feminism have taken a bit of distance from this "foundationalist" approach, but it continues to have a large following. Beyond feminism, we read in the writings of Hodgson substantive arguments of a deeply rooted current of thought describing the diffusion of Islam in the Arabian peninsula as historical progress for the rights of women, given what they had been before. But if Hodgson recognized that we lack trustworthy information on the social practices of the pre-Islamic periods, he took for his own, for example, the argument that the Muslim religion had put an end to infanticide, which particularly concerned girls (1:182).

Was Hodgson a feminist? His personal position, let's insist, is close to the nineteenth-century reformist feelings within Islam, positions clearly expressed and debated at the time and since then. As Hodgson always insisted, his historical analysis was resolutely based on the (utopian) vision of the sharia and on the ideal spirit of Islam of the foundational period: "Finally, in Sharʿî eyes a free woman was (in principle) almost as free as a man, despite some ties of dependency. The whole atmosphere of servility and secrecy, founded on the use of slave guards, was seriously alien to the Sharʿî sense of human dignity" (2:144).

Here we cannot fail to note a parallel between the inclusive position that was his in the matter of male homosexuality.

Homoeroticisms

The question of male homosexuality is even more controversial in Islamic societies today than the question of the status of women. But at the same time a series of recent works have contributed to strongly rewrite these polemical questions as history.[38] If Hodgson doesn't quite escape from some clichés in the historical literature that existed at the time he was writing relative to Muslim societies, or even homosexuality, he nonetheless demonstrates an astonishing analytical lucidity and a surprisingly up-to-date scientific understanding.

His contribution to these debates is, however, rarely or only briefly mentioned in the contemporary literature—by Khaled al-Rouayheb, for example, in a stimulating book on homosexuality.[39] In truth it would be demanding a lot from the Quaker who was Hodgson to be entirely open to varieties of sexuality other than heteronormative. We find in his analyses the old argument of a homosexuality "by default," the idea that the separation of the sexes, but also the difficulties of having access to the other sex in a highly segregated space, and the pressures deriving from this radical alternative, will inevitably produce a return to the same sex (*Venture* 2:145). This argument was notably developed by Abdelwahab Bouhdiba in his book *La sexualité en Islam*.[40] Significantly, this question is usually only treated from the male point of view. Avoiding in this way the orientalist cliché of lesbianism in the harem, Hodgson passes very modestly from the issue of women and their homo-relations, focusing his remarks on the issue of male homosexuality: "Complementary to the harem system was a conventional pattern of homosexual relations, especially among males, that sometimes became highly formal" (2:145).

Beyond this heteronormative reading, we find a series of arguments that remain current and pertinent. First, he underscores the character of a poetry that by convention was addressed to another man or to an ephebe as a way of respecting the space of honorability and modesty of women (*Venture* 2:303). Poetry, especially Persian poetry addressed by men to a masculine loved one, or to an ephebe, was in any event part of an aristocratic and aesthetic code (2:146).[41] Hodgson believed it right to specify that the sexual relations of an adult man with an adolescent were "probably anal" (2:145). The image of the lover and beloved in classical Athens was explicitly summoned up (2:145n87). It is only in a fortuitous manner that Hodgson mentions that singing slave girls were also present in the public space (1:343).

Elsewhere he strongly underscores, in a manner entirely in accord with the scientific beliefs of his time, the profoundly asymmetric character of these homoerotic relations. To be a *sabreur* or a *sabré* did not have the same meaning. On this point Hodgson opposes Islamic cases to the example of Sparta where, by sharing intimacy with an older man, a young boy acquired on the contrary a virile chastity (*Venture* 2:146).[42] As for the comparison of any passive male in a sexual act with a woman, Afsaneh Najmabadi has recently disputed this scheme, arguing that the penetrated man identified with an ephebe and not with a woman (2:146).[43]

This was an argument denied in a contemporary manner by David Ayalon and that Hodgson himself briefly formulated as the link between the emergence of a governing military class in the "Middle Periods" and homosexuality: "Perhaps the militarization of the highest social classes contributed to this with its stress on masculine society. It was especially in the Middle Periods, in association with the military courts of the amîrs, that sex between males entered pervasively into the ethic and the aesthetic of the upper classes" (*Venture* 2:145).

Even before these questions were discussed as they have been at least since Michel Foucault, in the light of homosexual identity and the "invention" of homosexuality, Hodgson described quite correctly the character of relations between men as being not exclusive and not productive of a distinct homosexual identity. Many of them, he noted, had wives and children: "It must be recalled that most of the men who, following fashion, had occasional relations with youths continued to be interested primarily in women and produced numbers of children" (*Venture* 2:146).

With a surprising confidence, he assures the reader that the famous ninth-century poet Abu Nuwas wrote poems for boys "without himself being homosexual." Hodgson recognized him as a libertine but not a homosexual: "Abû-Nuwas dedicated much of his erotic verse to the love of youths, thus settling a fashion that was later to become fixed in some Islamicate circles even if the poet had no personal homosexual interests" (*Venture* 1:297). This is a paradox for a figure who would become by the twentieth century absolutely emblematic of the homoerotic masculine heritage of all of Islamic culture.[44] It was as a lover of men and not as a libertine that Abu Nuwas was copiously censured in poetic anthologies at the beginning of the twentieth century, as is recalled as much by Khaled Rouayheb as by Joseph Massad. But he was also the cantor of the androgynous body and of girly-boys. Here, Hodgson grounded his interpretation on verses that the poet addressed to a serving girl or a concubine *ghulamiyya*, slave girl dressed as a boy, thereby confirming the pattern of nonexclusive sexualities, albeit with a marked preference for one or the other sex.[45] Hodgson's apparent objection to the homosexuality of Abu Nuwas seems pertinent in the sense that it "preformulates" up to a certain point the idea today at the center of debate, that the homosexual (or heterosexual) did not exist as such in these periods; men having relations with other men were not therefore in these contexts homosexual.

Thus, far from firmly clinging to the example of ancient Greece, the author attempts on the contrary to relativize rather than to endorse the trope of Islamic homosexuality, as a way of absolving Islamic societies.[46] We understand that the issues are at least as contemporary as they are historical, and that he is responding to present-day characterizations of Muslim societies as having homosexual tendencies. The frame of interpretation of these relations remains, let us insist, strictly heteronormative. The passive young boy is assimilated to a woman. But Hodgson's concern is not to ascribe to it any moral posture: neither condemnation nor tolerance (*Venture* 2:146).[47] It is just a question of understanding the social logics at work.

It must however be noted that beyond the same-sex relations (and whatever one understands by this) his reading of sexuality in Islamic societies is globally based upon the presupposition of fairly brutal drives, and not only in what concerns relations among men. The sexual act, in these contexts, is part of an act of domination for Hodgson. His characterization of the sexual act as a "masculine triumph" could not be clearer: "The tendency to see the sex act as the domination of male over female was sometimes exaggerated into the victory of the male over a subjected female" (*Venture* 2:142). One could ask to what documentary source exactly he is referring when he affirms, for example that girls are taught by their mothers how to sexually satisfy a man and to retain his affection (2:142). The result of this education appears not to be conclusive. In another passage he suggests a "hussar style" sexuality in which erotic games take but a rudimentary place, specifying between parentheses that the harem system certainly encouraged this trait (2:145).

This characterization of masculine authority as potentially brutal echoes to a degree his vision of military despotism as violent, and the relations between classes as taking place under the sign of brutality. The despotism of a great absolute monarch is an indifferent despotism in his characterization, while the personal arbitrariness of a man whose force resides in his perpetual vigilance and who is not very different socially from any other military chief is truly violent (*Venture* 2:131ff.). Although the mention of poetry, especially Persian poetry, refers to the context of love, the love of men among themselves, but also conjugal love, as well as elegies for a deceased spouse, the question of sexuality only evokes images of hasty and frustrating sexual unions (2:304). In Islamic literature of erotology, Hodgson keeps a form of simplicity as evidenced in his manner of evoking the body, sexual activity, or even sexual moods. However, his general perception of sexuality in Islamic societies takes place not under the sign of accomplishment, but rather of structural tension, which in an agreed manner proceeds in his eyes to polygyny.

It is thus that he tells with remarkable realism a tale from Rumi, the famous thirteenth-century Persian mystic, about the jealousy of women as a structuring principle of domestic cohabitation. A woman who was profoundly jealous of a beautiful slave girl kept watch so as not to ever leave her alone with her husband. But one day when she went to the baths, she sent her slave to the house to fetch something. Then, realizing her foolishness and returning quickly to her house, she discovered her husband with his clothing all askew, but who quickly upon being discovered assumed the prayer posture. His pretense was quickly revealed by the stains on his clothing, such that the wife slapped him and stuck out her tongue at him. The lesson of this tale, according to Hodgson, is that the obvious ritual impurity of the husband who was pretending to pray made his deceit a pathetic ruse and rendered him ridiculous (*Venture* 2:145).

The moral of this story is correct, but one can see also in the same anecdote an impertinent wink at the many tricks and allusions that took place in which the prayer posture is compared to the positions of having sex.[48] A similar lack of seriousness toward religion is hard to believe with Hodgson. His reading of questions about sexuality seem double, for sure, divided into a quite contemporary and puritan perception about sexual relations in Islamic societies (all questions about sex are shameful, he affirms),[49] and the banal naturalism of these cautionary tales, erotic or simply entertaining, that belong to a long literary tradition in Islam and to which he resorts as well, as we have seen, with a lack of self-consciousness.[50]

His reference to the sharia is in any event constant in a definition that is, it's true, reasonably idiosyncratic. Not that the egalitarian ideal in which he invests it is foreign to its acceptance in Islam, far from it.[51] But he systematizes this egalitarian principle in a very utopian way at all levels of social experience. At the heart of his historical approach, then, we find basically and in spite of everything a declinationist vision of the history of Islam.

Decline, in Spite of Everything?

It is paradoxical to wonder about the place of decline in the work of Marshall Hodgson when his entire approach is directly hostile to the notion of Islamic decadence (*Venture* 2:8). He writes forcefully (in an undeniable historiographical premonition, since today the idea of decline is vigorously opposed, notably in the context of Ottoman historiography): "In any case, the notion of Muslim decadence cannot be seriously maintained until the effect is eliminated of a variety of preconceptions and unbalanced procedures of inquiry that would be bound to produce the illusion of a relatively early decadence, whether there was decadence or not."[52]

It is delicious, moreover, to note that the implicitly essentialist title of Bernard Lewis's post-9/11 book *What Went Wrong?* appears to directly echo a question and a subtitle of Hodgson: "Westerners often ask what it was that went wrong, that the Muslim lands, once powerful, did not go on to share in the great Western transformations of the seventeenth and eighteenth centuries and enter modern times on a par with the Occident" (*Venture* 2:105).[53]

But we must place Hodgson's perspective in the context of the author of *The Venture of Islam*. At bottom it is "foundationalist," as has been suggested about his discussion of the woman question and original Islam. This is true even if Hodgson reveals a particular affinity for the medieval period ("the Middle Periods") in his reading of Irano-Semitic history, and for this moment when the political divisions of the great powers of the caliphs allowed the flowering of Islamic culture in its full expression. As far as the status of women is concerned, the Middle Periods were nonetheless a regressive moment with respect to the spirit of the sharia and the Muhammadan project, as well as in the example of the life of the Prophet. There we find the essentialization of the sharia, as formulated by E. Burke.[54] The secular decline of the Islamic world in the eighteenth century (discussed by Hodgson in volume 3 of *Venture*) would need to be rewritten as part of the long process of the devitalization of the ideals of the sharia.[55] Now the declinationist theme that Hodgson takes for his own account is especially relevant for him in light of a history of women and the feminine condition, although scarcely original.

The historiographical argument about the decline of the Islamic world—a commonplace of chroniclers forever—resonates with the moment when he wrote, with the developmentalist logics of the 1960s and the challenge of underdevelopment (from which it is impossible to escape except through a reform of the condition of women, according to the slogans of the period).[56] But the emphasis that Marshall Hodgson places upon the decline of women's freedom after the first Islamic centuries, and on the progressive abandonment or the twisting of the spirit of the sharia, takes us to the reformist spirit of the Arab Nahda, or Renaissance, of the nineteenth century. Hodgson refers to these debates with great conviction, especially the violent controversy set off by the Egyptian thinker Qasim Amin (*Venture* 3:288–89). The author of *The Venture of Islam* endorses some of the most stereotyped arguments of the twentieth-century modernists relative to the emancipatory reform of the Islam world and the woman question.

First, we find in his analyses a conventional vision of a global failure of the social order connected to the "harem system." After having underlined that women (at least in most periods) could be literate, knowledgeable teachers, the lack of education of women becomes for him a key element in his argument of social decadence, as many Muslim reformists affirmed at the beginning of the twentieth century. Barely educated, women were unable to conveniently educate their children, or to provide them with edifying examples, such that they were spoiled by their domestic servants or left to themselves: "Worse (as many have pointed out), a typical secluded woman could not give her sons, in their formative early years, the experience and guidance which would enable them to profit most fully from their later years of apprenticeship among the men. To the pampering that privileged children necessarily received from servants was too often added a petty and irresponsible direction from the mother" (*Venture* 2:134).

Second, and for the same reasons, women failed to become stable and sure companions for their husbands, supporting them in all their enterprises, as European spouses were supposed to do. Even more, Hodgson replies to this point with the kind of argument (today considered hackneyed) by which homosexuality was explained in the 1960s in the Arab world.[57] The lack of education of women would have made them poor life companions, such that the men preferred the company of other men.[58] "Not only those younger males who did not have access to free females and could not afford female slaves, but also married men with substantial resources would vary their sexual relations with a (perhaps too subservient?) female by having sexual relations with a (perhaps more spirited?) male, especially an adolescent" (*Venture* 2:145).

To this educational deficiency of the women's world overflowing into the whole of the social equilibrium, one must add another constitutive weakness, a structural instability deriving from polygamy. After having developed, here as well, a rationalist anthropological reading of polygyny, and after having analyzed it in a neutral and functionalist way, Hodgson also endorses a series of historiographical clichés (which remain still current). The cohabitation of women was a source of incessant jealousy that weakened the entire family cell and the household. Especially the theme of "harem intrigues," which was a current historiographical element in the interpretation of political crises, is a prism for the reading he adopts as his own (*Venture* 2:143–44). In a real inversion, the head of the family, the master of the house, would find himself a foreigner in his own home, expelled or marginalized in a women's world that Hodgson no longer describes as an ideal egalitarian juxtaposition of nuclear families, but as a world where women had power over other women and maneuvered as best they could to obtain privileges for their own children versus the children of other women. The idea of a veritable gynocracy in the domestic space was moreover adopted by Hodgson in his analyses, along with the idea of a universe in which women ruled over other women while excluding the master of the household from the reality of power: "If the male was dominant in the sex act, his dominance at home was sometimes very nearly reduced to that" (2:143).

At the summit of the social world, the harem system seriously and structurally weakened the political order. Many political crises, according to Hodgson, might be blamed on the jealousies of the harem. It is especially the Iranian case to which he applies a reference to the "harem intrigues," perhaps an echo of the *Siyaset Nameh* of Nizam ul-Mulk (eleventh century) and his diatribes against the women's interference in political affairs.[59] The examples mentioned, to be clear, refer to the world of the Safavids, but also to the Ottomans.

At the present moment a similar reductionism has barely been overcome in the historiography, but it was clearly featured at the heart of the developmentalist arguments in the 1960s and the debates about the Islamic world around polygyny. Marshall Hodgson's marked empathy for the positions of various Muslim reformists is clearly apparent in *Venture*, volume 3, book 6, and should not be confused with a Western external critique of the apathy or failure of societies of the Islamic world. It is remarkable to see how much in his reading of the question of conversions to Islam in sub-Saharan Africa—a thoroughly contemporary concern in an Africa still in the course of Islamization or Christianization, of "depaganization"—he rediscovers arguments attesting the idealization of the Islam of the early days.

In these pages in volume 3 of *Venture* he responds to quite Islamophobic arguments, explaining the spread of Islam in different parts of the world at the expense of Christianity, which experienced greater difficulty in its missionary enterprises (3:407ff.).[60] The increase in conversions to Islam was especially noticeable in sub-Saharan Africa. Hodgson cited Christian missionaries as explaining this disjuncture by asserting that Islam offered a greater doctrinal simplicity, which made it more accessible to "primitive" souls (3:408). He refutes this argument by noting the supposed obscurity of Christian mysteries and pagan myths, very similar according to him, while noting the opposite, the high degree of abstraction and theological difficulty of Muslim tradition on certain points. Closer to our current concerns especially, he replies to the other argument made by Christian missionaries, according to which the affinity of African pagans for Islam was the result of moral license authorized by the Muslim religion, notably its tolerance for polygamy.

To this point Hodgson develops the same argument that he includes in a clarifying note (*Venture* 1:340n12).[61] To distinguish, first of all, between a monogamous Christianity and a polygamous Islam appears illusory to him. Second, he disconnects these polygamous practices with a reference to the Quran, since Christian scriptural tradition, according to him, similarly authorized polygyny: "Monogamy is no more required, of ordinary believers, in the Bible than in the Qurʾân (and some Christian groups have allowed polygamy, as have even prominent Occidental theologians)" (3:408).

To conclude, on the question of gender, there is a double lesson. The author carries out an anthropological and historical decompartmentalization that scrambles the assumptions of specificity and closure, both cultural and theological. His demonstration is instantly applied to the comparisons, term by term, principally between the Christian Occident and the Islamic cultural area, and these in return are based upon the (same) fairly fixed, reified, and stereotyped social and cultural models.[62] What medieval historian would accept the caricatured vision of the Christian couple and family ("chivalric household") laid out by Hodgson, and applied to the entire Western world (*Venture* 2:64)? Who today would defend an approach so metonymic and totalizing of cultures, in which arabesques and cathedrals are presented as summarizing the essence of two opposed cultural systems?

It is nonetheless true that this idea of models and systems is still stimulating, anticipating disturbingly the issues and approaches today at the heart of the issues of gender: Muslim feminism, the debate over homosexual identity in the Islamic world (i.e., the idea that homosexuals should affirm a distinct identity).[63] The paradox is that his reading often adopts positions internal to Islam. In order to understand this interiority, this intimate taming of Islam, must one refer to Hodgson's personal life, to his Quaker beliefs, and to the affinities that he himself mentions between Christian and Muslim forms of abstinence, for example (*Venture* 2:408)?

It is a paradox that one can at least highlight. While contemporary historiography today shows a marked return as a kind of homage to Hodgson, many authors picking up the term "Islamicate" that he invented to express the civilizational character of Muslim society as it applied to non-Muslim subjects, it is nonetheless the question of religion, under the name of sharia, which is at the heart of and gives rise to his reading of Islamic history. In the open, extensive, and social definition that he gives the sharia, we are authorized to see, in our contemporary contexts, the point of view of a "moderate Islamist," or still more the theoreticians of Islamic feminism, or even the point of view of the theoreticians of the nineteenth-century Arab awakening, the Nahda, mentioned above, for the more dated aspects of the argument. As disorienting as the assumed interiority may be, it makes a good antiorientalist lesson, even more convincing when it draws upon questions of gender and sexuality which were at the heart of the orientalist project.

Is gender one of the most effective entry points from which to transform intellectual frontiers and to change periodizations? It appears to be a starting and deciding point but not in the sense that reformists and modernizers of all stripes since the nineteenth century, along with the colonial opponents of Islam and nationalist emancipators, had in mind in a disturbing consensus about the misery and alienation of Muslim women. Marshall Hodgson's approach succeeds at being at same time radically different, as when he inscribes himself in a global definition of gender relations at once global and transsocial. Despite his systematizations up to and including the ideal type, no culturalist withdrawal is radically imaginable in his perspective, since the classifications change instantly, and literally "common place" ideas arise at the time of thinking, and the Islamic world is never absolutely specific in his thought.

Might it be the case that questions relative to gender are more apt than others to act as levers, calling forth original periodic and geographic remappings. In their book, W. G. Andrews and M. Kalpakli ask us to see in the early modern period a "period" of love and lovers common to the Ottoman Empire and western Europe.[64] This work, while as fragile and debatable as Hodgson's approach, might in many ways confirm the centrality of the issue of gender as far as it is historicized and historically construed—thereby escaping an ahistorical, old-fashioned, and generally agreed-upon anthropology (so common when it comes to Islam). In the end, it is also true that neither gender nor sexuality is an autonomous space, nor are either categories outside of the social and political field.

Notes

I thank Robert Mankin and Edmund Burke for the great conference, and Edmund Burke for his patient translation of my chapter.

1. J. Dakhlia, "La culture nébuleuse ou l'Islam à l'épreuve de la comparaison," *Annales: Histoire, sciences sociales* 56 (2001): 1177–99.

2. Marshall G. S. Hodgson, *The Venture of Islam: Conscience and History in a World Civilization*, 3 vols. (Chicago: University of Chicago Press, 1974), 2:329–68 (hereafter cited in the text as *Venture*). For a French translation of this essay, see Abdesselam Cheddadi,

L'Islam dans l'histoire mondiale (Paris: Sindbad/Actes Sud, 1998), 103–73 (hereafter cited as Cheddadi trans.).

3. See E. Burke III, "Islamic History as World History: Marshall Hodgson, 'the Venture of Islam,'" *International Journal of Middle East Studies* 10 (1979): 241–64, 249, 256–57, and esp. 262: "However convincingly presented, this analysis contains the seeds of those same difficulties that Hodgson has rightly deplored in the work of others."

4. "On neither side was the contrast carried out fully in the Early Middle Period. Moreover, in some perspectives, the difference between the Occident and Islamdom dwindles to the accidental." Hodgson, *Venture,* 2:347; Cheddadi trans., 137.

5. See "Cultural Patterning," in *Venture,* 2:345; Cheddadi trans., 127–40, esp. 130ff.

6. Hodgson, *Venture,* 2:344; Cheddadi trans., 130.

7. Hodgson, *Venture,* 2:344; Cheddadi trans., 165.

8. Hodgson, *Venture,* 2:345; Cheddadi trans., 145.

9. Hodgson, *Venture,* 2:345; Cheddadi trans., 130–31.

10. Hodgson, *Venture,* 2:345; Cheddadi trans., 133.

11. See my "Du 'tapis maghrébin' au 'polygone étoilé': Retour sur le motif," *Revue des Mondes musulmans et de la Méditerranée* 83–84 (1997): 125–34.

12. Berque, cited in "Du 'tapis maghrébin,'" 129.

13. Hodgson, *Venture,* 2:345; Cheddadi trans., 133.

14. Hodgson, *Venture,* 2:348; Cheddadi trans., 138.

15. See E. Evans-Pritchard, *The Nuer: A Description of the Modes of Livelihood and Political Institutions of a Nilotic People* (Oxford: Oxford University Press, 1940); E. Gellner, *Saints of the Atlas* (London: Weidenfeld & Nicolson, 1969).

16. Marshall G. S. Hodgson, "The Role of Islam in World History," in *Rethinking World History: Essays on Europe, Islam, and World History,* ed. Edmund Burke III (Cambridge: Cambridge University Press, 1993), 115; and Cheddadi trans., 132.

17. Hodgson, *Venture,* 2:344–45; Cheddadi trans., 132.

18. Hodgson, *Venture,* 2:346; Cheddadi trans., 135.

19. Hodgson, *Venture,* 2:355; Cheddadi trans., 150–51.

20. Hodgson, *Venture,* 2:354; Cheddadi trans., 150.

21. All quotations in this paragraph are from Hodgson, *Venture,* 1:340n12.

22. "The nuclear family—man, wife and children—was stressed as a self sufficient unit, with every marriage given equal status at law," Hodgson, *Venture,* 1:181.

23. Here we can refer to the notable work of D. Ayalon, *Gunpowder and Firearms in the Mamluk Kingdom: A Challenge to Medieval Society* (London: Valentine, Mitchell, 1956), and all of the work of Ayalon on the articulation of the Harem and the Mamluks. On the Ottomans, see L. Peirce, *The Imperial Harem: Women and Sovereignty in the Ottoman Empire* (Oxford: Oxford University Press, 1993).

24. Hodgson, *Venture,* 2:355; Cheddadi trans., 151.

25. "The fashion of the wealthy tends to become the norm of those lower on the social scale," Hodgson, *Venture,* 1:341.

26. J. G. Peristiany, ed., *Honour and Shame: The Values of Mediterranean Society* (Chicago: University of Chicago Press, 1966).

27. Hodgson, *Venture,* 2:124n16. See G. Tillion, *Le Harem et les cousins* (Paris: Éditions

du Seuil, 1966); translated into English by Quintin Hoare as *My Cousin, My Husband: Clans and Kinship in Mediterranean Societies* (London: Saqi Books, 2007).

28. "[A]n institution which in its fullest form the Sharîàh could not wholly approve: the 'harem system,'" Hodgson, *Venture*, 2:143. See also ibid., 2:144, for the idea that the sharia might accept, even if it did not encourage, the recourse to slave concubines, albeit with certain limits.

29. Today the history of eunuchs is experiencing a strong renewal. Among others notably, see D. Ayalon, *Outsiders in the Lands of Islam: Mamluks, Mongols, and Eunuchs* (London: Variorum Reprints, 1988); Ayalon, *Eunuchs, Caliphs and Sultans: A Study in Power Relationships* (Jerusalem: Magnes Press, Hebrew University, 1999); and S. Marmon, *Eunuchs and Sacred Boundaries in Islamic Society* (Oxford: Oxford University Press, 1995).

30. P. Bourdieu, *Esquisse d'une théorie de la pratique précédé de Trois études d'ethnologie kabyle* (Geneva: Droz, 1972); Bourdieu, *Le sens pratique* (Paris: Éditions de Minuit, 1980).

31. E. K. Rowson, "The Effeminates of Early Medina," *Journal of the American Oriental Society* 111, no. 4 (1991): 671–93.

32. Hisham Sharabi, *Embers and Ashes: The Memoirs of an Arab Intellectual* (Boston: Olive Branch Press, 2008), 109–11.

33. Hodgson, *Venture*, 2:355; Cheddadi trans., 150.

34. On this question see notably G. Hambly, ed., *Women in the Medieval Islamic World: Power, Patronage and Piety* (New York: Palgrave, 1998).

35. Hodgson, *Venture*, 2:354; Cheddadi trans., 149.

36. From a considerable bibliography, we should note especially L. Ahmed, *Women and Gender in Islam: Historical Roots of a Modern Debate* (New Haven, CT: Yale University Press, 1992); M. Badran, "Toward Islamic Feminisms: A Look at the Middle East," in *Hermeneutics of Honor: Negotiating Female "Public" Space in Islamicate Societies*, ed. A. Afsaruddin (Cambridge, MA: Harvard University Press, 1999).

37. F. Mernissi, *The Veil and the Male Elite: A Feminist Interpretation of Women's Rights in Islam* (New York: Perseus, 1991); Mernissi, *Forgotten Queens of Islam* (New York: Policy Press, 1993). See R. Afshari, "Egalitarian Islam and Misogynist Islamic Tradition: A Critique of the Feminist Reinterpretation of Islamic History and Heritage," *Critique* 4 (1994): 13–33.

38. S. Schmidtke, "Homoeroticism and Homosexuality in Islam: A Review Article," *Bulletin of the School of Oriental and African Studies* 61 (1999): 260–66; J. Dakhlia, "Homoeroticisms and Historiographical Backgrounds of the Islamic World," *Annales: Histoire, sciences sociales*, no. 5 (September–October 2007): 1097–1120.

39. K. El Rouayheb, *Before Homosexuality in the Arab-Islamic World, 1500–1800* (Chicago: University of Chicago Press, 2005), 3; translated into French by Dimitri Kijek as *L'amour des garçons en pays arabo-islamique, XVIe–XVIIIe siècle* (Paris: Epel, 2010).

40. A. Bouhdiba, *La sexualité en Islam* (Paris: Presses Universitaires de France, 1975).

41. See W. G. Andrews and M. Kalpakli, *The Age of Beloveds: Love and the Beloved in Early-Modern Ottoman and European Culture and Society* (Durham, NC: Duke University Press, 2005).

42. See F. Lagrange, *Islam d'interdits, Islam de jouissance* (Paris: Téraèdre, 2008).

43. See also A. Najmabadi, *Women with Mustaches and Men without Beards: Gender and Sexual Anxieties of Iranian Modernities* (Berkeley: University of California Press, 2005).

44. On the emblematic role of Abu Nuwas, see especially El Rouayheb, *Before Homosexuality*; and J. Massad, *Desiring Arabs* (Chicago: University of Chicago Press, 2008); as well as the article by F. Lagrange in *The Encyclopedia of Gay Histories and Cultures*, ed. G. Haggerty (New York: Garland, 2000).

45. See P. Kennedy, *Abu Nuwas: A Genius of Poetry* (Oxford: Oneworld, 2005).

46. Najmabadi, *Women with Mustaches*.

47. See also J. Dakhlia, "Homoeroticisms."

48. See, e.g., the work of Frederic Lagrange on erotic humor in Arab literature.

49. "At the same time, the need for sexual privacy was exaggerated into a sense of shame about all things sexual." Hodgson, *Venture*, 2:142.

50. How can we explain that Hodgson can speak of "shame" with regard to all things relative to sex (*Venture*, 2:142) at the same time that he makes use of such narrative material?

51. See L. Marlowe, *Hierarchy and Egalitarianism in Islamic Thought* (Cambridge: Cambridge University Press, 1997).

52. Hodgson, "The Role of Islam in World History," 103.

53. See B. Lewis, *What Went Wrong? The Clash between Islam and Modernity in the Middle East* (New York: Harper, 2002); translated into French by Jacqueline Carnaud as *Que s'est-il passé? L'Islam, l'Occident et la modernité* (Paris: Gallimard, 2002).

54. Burke, "Islamic History."

55. See especially "Before the Deluge: The Eighteenth Century," in Hodgson, *Venture*, 3:134ff.

56. J. Dakhlia, *Le divan des rois: Le politique et le religieux dans l'Islam* (Paris: Aubier, 1998).

57. D. Zeevi, *Producing Desire: Changing Sexual Discourse in the Ottoman Middle East, 1500–1900* (Berkeley: University of California Press, 2006).

58. "The advice of women kept in seclusion was, in any case, not such as to inspire their men with magnanimity, or event to curb them with practical good sense." Hodgson, *Venture*, 2:144.

59. On the political intrigues of the harem, see especially Hodgson, *Venture*, 2:144. Also ibid., 3:56, 103, 117, 127.

60. In recent decades conversion to Christianity is again expanding.

61. See also *supra* n. 23.

62. The comparison is initially with the Chinese and Hindu systems, but subsequently narrows to the system of oppositions between Islam and Christianity. Hodgson, *Venture*, 2:64–65. Also J. Dakhlia, "La culture nébuleuse."

63. S. Amer, "Joseph Massad and the Alleged Violence of Human Rights," *GLQ: A Journal of Lesbian and Gay Studies* 16, no. 4 (2010): 649–53.

64. Andrews and Kalpakli, *Age of Beloveds*.

CHAPTER NINE

The Problem of Muslim Universality

Faisal Devji

Race and civilization constituted the two global categories of imperialism as a form of knowledge. For whatever their intellectual antecedents in Europe, these categories had been deployed and become familiar in Asian and African societies as part of the history of European dominance, if not colonialism, there. Indicative of such a context was the fact that while these terms were global, insofar as their reality extended beyond the political borders of any state, they were at the same time deprived of universality. Instead, they represented global visions of hierarchy and exclusion that were often described in the language of anxiety, perhaps because they couldn't be anchored in any political institutions (thus the counterfactual if commonplace European laments, starting in the nineteenth century, about the decline of Western civilization or the subordination of the Aryan race). Such institutions, after all, were still defined by particular states, singly or in combination, which stood then and now as the foundations of the international order. As global categories lacking institutional foundations, then, race and civilization sometimes took very direct and visceral forms, such as fear, violence, or discrimination, which might not have possessed any legal sanction.

Now, as global categories race and civilization may well have allowed Europeans or Americans to think about the ambiguous relationship between their own national and imperial states, as well as about the emergence of a new political arena lacking institutional foundations that the latter made possible. For colonized intellectuals, however, or those who were faced by the apparently insurmountable dominance of "the West," these categories were more often than not the sites of great struggles that were directed along quite different lines. For these individuals sought to reject the hierarchies of race, even as they sometimes tried to come to terms with the apparently more benign exclusions of civilization, if only by asserting their own status within such categories. These men, in other words, were not simply occupied with the determination to protect their own race, religion, or civilization from the transformations of colonial rule, but, conversely, with defending universal ideas of equality and freedom well beyond their European peers.

Far more than their metropolitan contemporaries, therefore, such intellectuals and men of action not only questioned the categories of imperial knowledge by pointing out their self-justifying parochialism, which reserved a large number of rights and freedoms for the exclusive use of those who possessed the appropriate racial or civilizational attributes; they also sought to demonstrate the universality of their own supposedly nonracial and tolerant or egalitarian civilizations, often understood as mirror images of some European one. But more than this, many of them also fought to free Europe's own liberal heritage from the racial and civilizational prejudices of its owners, and so to fulfil what they considered its inherent universality in a truly global way, by stripping it of any particular civilizational heritage.

Gandhi was only the most famous of many such thinkers, struggling early in his career to redeem the British Empire by democratizing it into the first truly global political order, one whose sheer diversity would not allow it to be founded on any single race, nation, or civilization.[1] Even after he relinquished this extraordinarily universal vision of liberal politics, which, unlike that of liberalism's founding figures, didn't consign colonial subjects to what the historian Dipesh Chakrabarty has called the "waiting room of history,"[2] Gandhi refused to base a political order on any ascribed identity. Indeed, he noted that such global identities as race and civilization had assumed political importance only once they had in fact been stripped of reality. For the universalization of consumption as a cultural form emerging out of industrialism, he held, suggested that modern civilization no longer had any need of something called "the West," which it simply commoditized, used, and spat out in its seemingly inexorable march to world dominance. And against this Gandhi proposed not some alternative universality, but instead its radical destruction as a form.[3]

These claims for equality and universality, as also their subjection to criticism, had characterized colonial intellectuals and politicians from the late nineteenth century. Once the European empires were gradually wound up after World War II, however, it was a newly constituted "West," led by the United States, that came to represent a universal mission in an equally new global arena defined by the Cold War. Whether identified with modernization theory, development, or, with particular reference to the Soviet bloc, democracy, this universality also claimed to be free of race or civilization, though such categories continued to play a role in the domestic politics of European and American states, particularly where minority and immigrant groups were concerned. It was now left for those in the newly independent countries of Asia and Africa to cast doubt on the universality of modernization, development, or even democracy as purveyed by the "West."

It was this apparently hegemonic vision of what he described as the "technicalistic" universality of our global present that Marshall Hodgson took as the starting point of his study of Islamic civilization, seen as a form of universality anterior to it. In doing so, of course, he harked back to thinkers like Husserl or Heidegger (to say nothing of Gandhi), who from the period following World War I had been concerned with the nature of technological universality and its consequences for European civilization. But as I will argue here, Hodgson was also interested in the non-Western and indeed colonial history of this phenomenon, as well as in what resources it might offer to mitigate the harmful effects of "technicalism" as the form of universality that he thought defined all modern life. More than a history of Islamic civilization, then, or even a comparative or world history, Hodgson's intellectual project in *The Venture of Islam* might be seen as providing us with a non-Western genealogy of modernity and our global present.

Dead Civilizations

Despite its richness, therefore, Hodgson's account of world history as a history of civilizations, and Islamic civilization in particular, has the character of a postmortem examination. Indeed from the viewpoint of what he saw as the global present, defined in terms of a general civilizational un-grounding and borderless-ness, the history of civilizations was dead:

> By the twentieth century, though the Islamic allegiance continues strong in most regions where Islam had once come to prevail, these Muslim regions no longer form a single society with a common ongoing cultural tradition, but rather are severally articulated into a wider world society, the institutions of which have largely been evolved in the Occident. Moreover, in that new world society, no longer agrarianistic in its dominant sectors, all the cultural heritages from agrarianistic times, including even the Occidental heritage itself, have been put in question; still more so, then, that associated with Islam.[4]

Hodgson even seems to reject what has become his most influential category, the Islamicate, which, like the term Italianate from which it was fashioned, suggested the expansion of some particular form into a larger, if more general, civilizational entity no longer tied to any specific country or religion. Thus he noted the reemergence of religion among Muslims in the twentieth century as the sole referent of the term "Islam," one whose more expansive civilizational form has been dissolved in the global present that, I will argue, was defined for Hodgson by the Cold War. "The most significant element of the Islamic heritage now," he wrote, "is religion and the religious conscience. Religion is again now, as in the first generation of Muslims, the core of the community heritage—so far as that does actively survive; it is the effective residue of the centuries of Islamicate evolution" (*Venture* 3:412).

What interested Hodgson about Islamic civilization as a potentially universal form was not only the possibility it offered of constructing a genealogy of the global present, whose absence he thought was what made it literally unthinkable and so sublime in its technological dominance, but also of imagining an alternative trajectory of the global. To begin with, then, Hodgson thought that the memory and detritus of potentially universal civilizations like Islam, but also the lived reality of religions more generally, permitted them to mediate and ground the global present, if only because they represented older ideas of universality: "The basis of community allegiance needs to be reformulated in a society where the religious community is but one of several, none serving as foundation for their common culture. There are many possibilities; I shall suggest one: in such a world, religious communities may play a crucial role, that of communities intermediate between the individual and the global mass of four billions, all potentially watching the same television programmes and buying the same products" (*Venture* 3:433–34).

For Hodgson, however, Islam was especially important because it provided the only universal form that civilization took before the global present inaugurated by the West, thus serving both as its antecedent and alternative. This is clear from his use of the thoroughly abstract and indeed nontopographical terms "hemisphere" and "hemispheric" to describe Islamic civilization, as much as the political divisions of the global present:

> Until the seventeenth century of our era, the Islamicate society that was associated with the Islamic religion was the most expansive society in the Afro-Eurasian hemisphere and had the most influence on other societies. This was in part because of its central location, but also because in it were expressed effectively certain cultural pressures—cosmopolitan and egalitarian (and anti-traditional)—generated in the older and more central

> lands of this society. The culture of Islamdom offered a norm of international sophistication to many peoples as they were being integrated into this hemispheric commercial nexus. It also offered a flexible political framework for increasing numbers of long-civilized peoples.[5]

As a political category, the hemisphere possesses a strongly American genealogy, dating from the Monroe Doctrine's claim to hemispheric dominance in the Americas and over much of the Pacific, and including the Cold War distinction between the eastern and western hemispheres. It was with the Monroe Doctrine, after all, that the globe became a political arena for the first time, the space it demarcated having become abstract insofar as it abjured territory altogether for longitudes and latitudes that passed through the middle of oceans, and whose hemisphere distinguished the New World from the Old. The Cold War had similarly redefined the terms "east" and "west" as abstract global categories. Since a hemisphere has no geographical, or rather topographical, boundaries, it could therefore shift easily from the Monroe Doctrine's definition, which distinguished between the Old and New Worlds, to one that bundled Western Europe and the Americas together against the Soviet Union and its allies.[6]

America was also crucial for Hodgson's definition of civilizational universality because he thought that only its discovery and colonization permitted Europe to outstrip the Islamic world economically, politically, and indeed geographically, to constitute itself as "the West" for the first time in a geopolitically serious way. It is not accidental that the appropriation of the Americas for Western civilization occurs, in Hodgson's view, at the same time as what he calls "Islamdom's" own achievement of a civilizational rather than purely political or even religious universality, with its expansion beyond the "Irano-Semitic" tradition that had also defined earlier empires and civilizations. In both cases the achievement of a global and potentially universal order happens quite late, in the sixteenth century, well after the founding moments that Muslims and Westerners themselves tended to prize:

> By the sixteenth century, when the Muslim society extended far beyond the original Irano-Semitic limits, new sorts of institutions were arising. But at least till then no parochial corporate entity was allowed a permanent status, neither castes as in India nor estates and municipalities as in the Occident—even guilds were relatively weak. Nor was any bureaucratic state administration allowed to gain too great a predominance, as in Byzantium or China. By way of individual ties of contract and of patronage,

> governed by a common universal law to which all Muslims were subject wherever they might be found, urban society proceeded on its own, with a minimum of reliance on the garrisons in which ultimate power rested but whose chief essential function was to prevent bloodshed among rival factions within the towns. (*Rethinking* 117)

We might see echoes of Cold War concerns and, indeed, American ideals in this description of Muslim universality, where sovereign power is located outside urban life-worlds in garrisons; individual freedoms, contractually exercised, are not subordinated to corporate control; and the state is unable to dominate society because it has no real power over the sacred law. But while this vision might offer comfort to Muslim liberals and Islamists alike, Hodgson's insistence on the non–Middle Eastern or rather Mediterranean character of Islam's universality, with its dismissal of teleological accounts of the religion's greatness, does exactly the reverse:

> One natural but unfortunate tendency that has effectively molded our conceptions of Islamdom has been our concentration on the Mediterranean Muslim lands, since they were nearest to the Occident. Once this meant focussing on the Ottomans as they entered European diplomatic history; more recently, it has highlighted the peoples now using the Arabic language, in part because of a philological interest in the language and in classical "origins." A popular identification of Muslims with Arabs has resulted in an especially pervasive series of misperceptions. In fact, the most creative centers of Islamdom were, in all periods, mostly eastward from the Mediterranean—from Syria to the Oxus basin (and largely in non-Arab territory). (*Rethinking* 102)

Indeed he condemned contemporary Muslim attitudes to their past as being themselves the result of Western interpretations of the religion, which had always stressed the importance of its "classical" and "orthodox" history. If anything, then, contemporary Muslim views of early Islamic *history* (as opposed to premodern references to foundational *texts* in order to anchor juridical interpretation) betrayed a kind of mimicry of European ideas about the authenticity and continuing fecundity of history's founding moments. Or, as Hodgson put it, "another source of misconceptions has been the tendency of Muslims themselves, since the nineteenth century, to reject the immediate past as a failure and look to certain earlier 'classical' strands in their heritage that seem to offer resources against modern Western encroachments; a tendency that Westerners have often encouraged for their own reasons" (*Rethinking* 102).

Given the heavily medieval and Middle Eastern focus of Islamic history in Hodgson's day, as to some degree in our own, this expansion of the horizon was so novel as to be radical; but let us remember that it served to complement a similar shift in his view of the West, for whose universality America, and therefore the postmedieval world, was crucial. The role played by the Americas in the making of the West, in other words, was in "Islamdom" performed by South and Central Asia and sub-Saharan Africa. In both cases the geography and temporality of civilizational origins was displaced to make for a history capable of bringing together ostensibly different civilizations into a new kind of global genealogy. Rather than serving merely to illustrate the expansionary fate of seamless and continuous civilizations, in other words, Hodgson proposed the occurrence of a fundamental geographical, but also political and so conceptual break in the sixteenth century, one that made it possible to see "Islamdom" as a precursor of, and defeated alternative for, a new kind of global history.

The Future of an Illusion

Hodgson's account of the premodern, or rather precolonial, Muslim past is dominated by the kind of synthetic narrative and large-scale material factors, such as urbanization, agrarian economies, state formation, and the like, that still characterize world history. It is only when he comes to the colonial period that ideas assume a certain prominence in their own right, at least in part because he can now rely upon Muslim thinkers who, like him, are capable of writing about Islam and its mediating potential for our "technicalistic" age in a self-consciously modern and indeed global way. Of these intellectuals, the chief one is Muhammad Iqbal (d. 1938), an Indian poet and philosopher who even today is considered by many to be the most important thinker of modern Islam. Hodgson not only used Iqbal to ventriloquize his own ideas, but as I hope to show, also and equally voiced many of the Indian writer's thoughts as his own.

Writing as he did in Persian as well as in Urdu and English, and read well beyond his own country, Iqbal represented, in some sense, the possibility of Islam's global future; but as an Indian he might also have illustrated the fact that such a universality still possessed non–Middle Eastern sources. For Hodgson, in any case, Iqbal was the key thinker of modern Islam, situating it in a global history as part of the human heritage and seeking, like Hodgson himself, perhaps, to grasp modernity as a spiritual rather than merely "technicalistic" phenomenon. All this he was seen as doing at least in part through the theologically crucial idea of prophetic finality, which made Muhammad into a self-abrogating figure, the last major instance of a civilizational founder who relied upon premodern forms of knowledge that were based on occult forms of authority like revelation.[7]

By putting an end to his own role, Iqbal maintained, and in the process disdaining miracles and other supernatural forms of prowess, Muhammad made Islam into a future-oriented faith that took mankind and not God as its object, not least because the finality of prophethood meant that there could no longer be any direct communication or even mediation between man and God, with the former becoming for the first time the real agent of history. In Hodgson's words, "Muhammad's revelation was the final and most perfect revelation precisely in that it brought to mankind the principles which made further revelation superfluous" (*Venture* 3:349).

In some sense, of course, this vision belonged in the same intellectual tradition as Nietzsche's "death of God," and indeed the German philosopher was a major influence on the Indian thinker, though he repudiated or at least revised the former's apparent atheism. For Iqbal, the death of God, accomplished by the finality of prophecy and the coming to maturity of humanity as a historical actor in its own name, also marks the birth of what he called the Ultimate Individual. "The whole cosmos presented, in its totality, an absolute uniqueness: it expressed the individuality of the Absolutely Unique Individual, to be identified with what Islam knew as God. The destiny to which each finite individual, each human being, was called was to be more and more like God: more and more uniquely individual, and therefore more and more creative" (*Venture* 3:348).

One can see how Iqbal's individualistic interpretation of Islam might have appealed to Hodgson's own view of "Islamdom's" historical individualism, as distanced from Indian castes as it was from European guilds—though it is curious why he refused to consider the equally plausible link between the rules of caste and those of the sharia as forms of nonstate authority that gave both civilizations their integrity. Nevertheless, he thought Iqbal's project to be a magnificent failure, in part because the Indian writer was too seduced by the lure of origins and Islam's Mediterranean past. But Hodgson also thought that Iqbal sought to cut Islam off from the wider society of his own country, despite his theoretical claims regarding its synthetic character and focus on humanity.

What Hodgson was referring to, of course, was the poet-philosopher's idea of redistributing India into religiously defined provinces, which later allowed him to be appropriated by the Pakistan movement, as well as his support of conservative Muslim practices more generally.

Iqbal's conservatism was justified as part of a defensive and purely tactical—rather than principled—maneuver to protect a minority group in the new arena of mass politics that nationalism had brought into being in India under Gandhi's leadership. And Hodgson seemed to recognize that it was precisely the pragmatic and political nature of these moves, shielded as they were from Iqbal's avowed principles, which ended up betraying them. The Indian thinker, then, had reduced his vision of universality to a merely communal one, and though Hodgson did not mention it, an egregious instance of this was Iqbal's attempt to exclude a group called the Ahmadis from the Muslim communion, by claiming on very uncertain grounds that they denied the finality of prophecy, and so the emergence of humanity as the globe's only historical actor, by attributing semidivine status to their nineteenth-century founder.[8]

By sequestering Islam from his country's national movement, and thus from his own Hindu neighbors as well, Iqbal refused to recognize how Indian history might well provide Muslims with a model for their future as a global entity. Here Hodgson drew upon a famous speech of Iqbal's, in which the thinker had claimed that India, home to the world's largest Muslim population, was more important to Islam's future than all the lands occupied by his coreligionists put together. This was not due to the mere number of India's Muslims, but because they comprised at the same time a scattered and diverse minority, whose unity was thus not predicated upon any racial, cultural, political, or other commonality but one that was potentially universal.[9]

For Iqbal, therefore, India provided a demonstration of Islam as what he called a "people-building force," because it was an idea or view of the world rather than language, ethnicity, and the like that united Muslims with one another. But this also made India, for all her people, into Asia if not the world in miniature, and Iqbal hoped that if a political solution to the problem of diversity in the age of nationalism could be found there, it would resolve the political problem of Asia as a whole. "For Islam forms in principle a single worldwide society. And in the world as a whole the Muslims are, as in the more local case of India, distributed among a non-Muslim majority. The problem of the Muslims of India was in the end the problem of the Muslims in the world" (*Venture* 3:333).

Hodgson extended this line of thinking to India even after her partition, speculating that the country's still-enormous Muslim population might serve as a model in miniature for Islam as a global entity. "One would like to suppose that Muslims placed in a situation like that of the Muslims of the Indian Union might take the lead in such an endeavour. . . . The Muslims of the Indian Union find themselves, within the bounds of one national state, in a position which all Muslims occupy in reality (if less visibly) in the world at large—for the Muslims of the world likewise form a scattered minority in a world society they cannot control" (*Venture* 3:440).

A Shared Secret

More than merely following up some of Iqbal's ideas, Hodgson can be said to share an intellectual trajectory with him. Indeed, it is remarkable how the Indian writer's formulations, even in Hodgson's telling, aligned so well with those defining *The Venture of Islam*. A small and initial example of this can be seen in the way in which both men situated Islam's universality in its mediating, or what Iqbal might call "synthetic," role among the Old World's civilizations, which we have already observed Hodgson describe, in negative fashion, as being wary of India's castes as much as of Europe's guilds. How familiar, then, was his account of Iqbal being "assured that Islam contrasted both to a system like Hinduism, which possessed only the principle of continuity, and to a system like that of the Modern West which, because of crucial weaknesses in a Christianity which had rejected the Law, now possessed only the principle of development" (*Venture* 3:351).

Both men are known in their later work for stressing the importance of sacred law as the connecting thread making Muslim universality possible in premodern times, the question for contemporary Muslim thinkers being how to render it more flexible without snapping that thread. Yet both had begun their intellectual careers with major works that took exactly the opposite view, to focus on the crucial role of esotericism in the universalization of Islam. Whether it is Iqbal's doctoral thesis from Munich, *The Development of Metaphysics in Persia*, or Hodgson's only monograph, *The Secret Order of Assassins*, these texts might well represent each man's principal scholarly contribution, rather than the undergraduate textbook that is *The Venture of Islam* or the lectures to a lay audience collected as *The Reconstruction of Religious Thought in Islam*.

Although it had already become common to dismiss Iqbal's early work as immature, or consign it to an early and imperfect period of his understanding,

Hodgson saw clearly that despite his various statements criticizing Sufism as the chief form that esotericism took in Muslim history, Iqbal's work continued to be dominated by it:

> But his own outlook made use of ways of understanding Islam which the Sufis had made acceptable. He was more concerned with the inner spirit of Muhammad's revelation than with its outer detail; moreover, he looked to exceptional individuals to embody this spirit in their own lives on behalf of the community at large. When he cited justificatory parallels to his thought within the Islamic tradition, it was preponderantly from Sufi writers. (*Venture* 3:348–49)

> Such an historical role presupposed, as had Sufism, a special, creative role for a spiritual elite. It was the exceptional individual who, indeed, was the chief beneficiary of the principle of development and of freedom in Islam; it was through such individuals that history moved, greater individuality and variety were expressed, and the fullness of God's potentialities approached. Such individuals were on the way to becoming what Nietzsche had called the Superman, and what Iqbal described in classical Sufi terms as the Perfect Man, the end of creation and even its reason for existence. As had been the case with Sufism, though such an individual might see beyond the current form of the Shariah to possible future, better social forms, he was bound to uphold the Shariah as it stood meanwhile for the sake of social solidarity; for the masses could not be expected to understand truths on such a level. (*Venture* 3:350)

And if Iqbal continued to rely upon Islam's esoteric tradition, Hodgson thought it was because esotericism had provided the chief mode by which premodern Muslims could claim universality, representing therefore the only inheritance that Islam could offer in mediating the global present. And yet while it was inescapable, esotericism was also woefully inadequate to the task that confronted it:

> Those Muslims of the past who acknowledged this responsibility and yet responded to the human demand for a more universalistic outlook commonly cast their wider response into esoteric form, thus leaving the exoteric communalism untouched—but deprived of much of its power. But we have noted that during the nineteenth century most Muslims came to

> reject the conventional esoteric approaches to the problem, believing that the Muslim heritage could not be effectively defended without a more rigorous common discipline than esotericism encouraged; nor is esotericism congenial to the temper of a technicalistic world in which every idea and every standpoint is subject to repeated public investigation without respect for authority. A more dynamic way must be found for resolving the tension between universalism and communalism if Islamic communities—or, indeed, any other such intermediate communities—are to play the creative role in the world which they might. (*Venture* 3:435)

We are not told what this "more dynamic way" of mediating between the universal and particular might look like, but given his acknowledgment of Iqbal's disavowed, and so all the more powerful, esotericism, is it possible to think of Hodgson, too, engaging in such an exercise? The idea of a "secret writing" would surely have been familiar enough to Hodgson, not only from his own monograph on the Assassins, to say nothing of his work on Sufism and Islamic philosophy more generally, but particularly due to its celebrated and controversial elaboration by Leo Strauss, his colleague in the Committee on Social Thought at the University of Chicago, who himself relied heavily upon the work of Muslim philosophers like Farabi. And in fact Hodgson cited Strauss's views on Farabi, as well as his argument about secret writing, approvingly in the first volume of *Venture* (1:435n9).

While the link between Hodgson's views and those of Strauss is for the moment a speculative one, it is worth noting that the latter had tried to recast esotericism in the terms of political philosophy and to demonstrate its continuing relevance to modern times. I will argue below that Hodgson, too, came to see esotericism as crucial to Islam's future as a mediator of the universal. And so it is not insignificant that Hodgson (or the editor who completed his work posthumously) saw it fit to end the third and final volume of *Venture* with the following passage, in which the future of Islam is predicated upon an esoteric literary genre, famously associated with Sufism and described as a "secret leaven" within an ostensibly secular world:

> It is possible that eventually Islam (like Christianity already in some circles) will prove to have its most creative thrust by way of the great "secular" literature in which its challenge has been embedded, and will move among its heirs like a secret leaven long after they have forgotten they were once Muslims. Persian poetry will not die so soon as the disquisitions of fiqh

> or kalam. And Persian poetry may eventually prove to be as potent everywhere as among those who use language touched by the Persianate spirit, and so by Islam. (*Venture* 3:441)

Whether or not Hodgson indulged in the kind of secret writing that Strauss and perhaps even Iqbal did, he was convinced that unlike its premodern attempt at universality, for which the sacred law was so crucial, Islam's future engagement with the universal could only be of an inward kind. Thus while acknowledging the importance that social relations had come to have in modern interpretations of the Quran, he warned that "they must find ways of understanding and renewing Muslims' experience of the Quran as a vehicle of the inward life at the same time as they renew their response to the Quran as a guide to social relations" (*Venture* 3:440). This was not because religion had now to be confined to the inner life in some conventionally liberal way, but rather because the global political arena brought into being by the Cold War permitted neither the absolute dominance of one moral or political vision nor even an order standing alongside it as some kind of alternative:

> By the mid-twentieth century, the various Muslim peoples were having to face internally, as were the Westerners, the profound long-term effects of the nuclear aspects of the Great Transmutation, of technicalistic society and all the opportunities and dangers it opened up. But the Muslims' independent responsibility has been at the same time increasingly limited by the same conditions that limit that of the most technicalized nations: their new responsibility is increasingly a joint responsibility with the rest of mankind for common human problems. (*Venture* 3:413)

> Iqbal rather hoped that the Muslims could wait for the West to destroy itself and then take the West's place in world leadership, thus fulfilling the mission which already the Quran had indicated to them. Such a notion has lost any plausibility since 1945. If the West destroys itself, either physically or morally, it will hardly perish alone. (*Venture* 3:430)

And so we return to a conception of the world, or rather the Cold War's global arena, as India writ large, where Muslims, like all other peoples, must recognize they are a minority whose task is to mediate the global present as part of the joint work of humanity. It is precisely because of its outward or "technicalistic" character that our global present can and must be grasped or grounded in the inner life, thus giving it existential depth as much as moral meaning. But in casting off the esoteric dimension of its premodern universality, and stressing the external one of law instead, Islam was disabled from engaging in any serious way with a modernity that Iqbal had insisted needed to be understood spiritually, by breaking up its external character. In these circumstances, both Iqbal and Hodgson, I want to claim, returned to their early work on esotericism, whether or not they did so by way of a secret writing.

The Beginning in the End

The first important and sustained arguments that Iqbal and Hodgson made were in their doctoral theses, both of which were published as monographs to become influential texts that have been in print almost continuously ever since. Both books were concerned with the role of esotericism in the religious, philosophical, and political movements of Iran. They also focused in particular on the medieval heresy (or dissident movement, as Hodgson would have it) of the Nizaris, a group belonging to the Ismaili branch of the Shiʿa, who went the furthest in trying to instantiate a political order premised upon esotericism, one that entailed the suspension or even abolition of the sacred law. Hodgson cited Iqbal's *Development of Metaphysics in Persia* approvingly, if briefly, in *Venture*, and though it is a much shorter work than his own encyclopedic one, both texts were equally ambitious and wide-ranging.

Iqbal described the *Development* as a synthetic work, but also as one that offered the first systematic philosophical analysis of Sufism. The book is concerned with the struggle of Persian thought to ground and internalize the external world within the self, a task that, not coincidentally, also defined Iqbal's own work, not least his attempt to comprehend the spiritual character of modernity. And this is to say nothing about Hodgson's idea that the "technicalistic" character of the global present required grounding in the inner life if it was to be grasped and, as it were, spiritualized. In ancient Persia, claimed Iqbal, this struggle was manifested in the dualism of light and darkness, with the "negative" category represented by the latter constituting the principle of movement in this thinking.

With the coming of Islam, and the victory of Greek thought that Iqbal thought it had made possible, Persia had to grapple with the new externality of Semitic revelation, in addition to the Greek dualism of subject and object. It was the absorption of this dual challenge that allowed her to redefine Islam as a universal phenomenon, one whose forms of internalization included monism, pantheism, and idealism:

> The political revolution brought about by the Arab conquest marks the beginning of interaction between the Aryan and the Semitic, and we find that the Persian, though he lets the surface of his life become largely semitised, quietly converts Islam to his own Aryan habits of thought. In the West the sober Hellenic intellect interpreted another Semitic religion—Christianity; and the results of interpretation in both cases are strikingly similar. In each case the aim of the interpreting intellect is to soften the extreme rigidity of an absolute law imposed on the individual from without; in one word it is an endeavour to internalise the external.[10]

> The Persian mind, having adjusted itself to the new Political environment, soon reasserts its innate freedom, and begins to retire from the field of objectivity, in order that it may come back to itself and reflect upon the material achieved in its journey out of its own inwardness. With the study of Greek thought, the spirit, which was almost lost in the concrete, begins to reflect and realise itself as the arbiter of truth. Subjectivity asserts itself, and endeavours to supplant all outward authority. Such a period, in the intellectual history of a people, must be the epoch of rationalism, scepticism, mysticism, heresy—forms in which the human mind, swayed by the growing force of subjectivity, rejects all external standards of truth.[11]

It was in this situation of intellectual flux that the Ismailis emerged as an antinomian movement in Islamic history. Their emergence represented a paradox, for the intellectual freedom the Ismailis attained by spiritualizing the law ended up reducing external or received authority to a single point, embodied in the person of the Shiʿa imam, but by the same token making it all important. So it was now authority that had become the "negative" principle of movement (or development, as Hodgson would put it) that must be spiritualized. Iqbal traced the history of this spiritualization by looking at Ismailism's Sufi heirs, especially the mystical figure of the Perfect Man, ending with the Babi movement as an Ismaili form, and also as the culmination of Persian metaphysics: "In the Ismailian movement, Free thought, apprehending the collapse of its ever widening structure, seeks to rest upon a stable basis, and, by a strange irony of fate, is led to find it in the very idea which is revolting to its whole being. Barren authority, though still apt to reassert itself at times, adopts this unclaimed child, and thus permits herself to assimilate all knowledge past, present and future."[12]

One reason why Babism was so much like Ismailism was because, unlike Sufism, for the most part, it refused to confine esotericism to the inner life, but made it into something that was socially revolutionary. And this Iqbal saw as a risky but also positive thing, and he was even willing to attribute the political reforms of contemporary Persia to it: "But pure speculation and dreamy mysticism undergo a powerful check in Babism which, unmindful of persecution, synthesizes all the inherited philosophical and religious tendencies, and rouses the spirit to a consciousness of the stern reality of things. Though extremely cosmopolitan and hence quite unpatriotic in character, it has yet had a great influence over the Persian mind. The unmystic character and practical tone of Babism may have been a remote cause of the progress of recent political reforms in Persia."[13]

It is from Babism that Iqbal takes the Quranic justification for one of his most important claims, that man is God's partner, and his interest in Ismailism also had to do with it as the most radical form taken by this partnership—particularly in the heretical figure of the imam as a god-man. It was not, in other words, the Christian emphasis on God becoming mortal, but an Ismaili or Sufi concern with man becoming divine that interested Iqbal: "The god-man is he who has known the mystery of his own being, who has realised himself as god-man; but when that particular spiritual realisation is over, man is man and God is God. Had the experience been permanent, a great moral force would have been lost and society overturned."[14]

It should be clear that the radical themes of Iqbal's early interests are all to be found in his later work, except with the heretical references removed. But whether it was medieval Persia or modern Islam, his concern was to understand how the external world could be grasped spiritually, and in so doing universalize the self and make it divine. The same might be said for Hodgson's project in *The Venture of Islam*, which arguably drew upon the argument he'd made in *The Secret Order of Assassins*, in which he described Islamic history as a conflict between two forms of universality. The Sunni one was fundamentally conservative, based on a historical inheritance made up of scripture, prophetic tradition, and the sacred law, while the Ismaili was radical because founded upon human reason directed into the future. Ismailism, then, entailed the subordination of everything that had been inherited to the intellect and so to man:

> For not only do men, as microcosm, represent all realms of being; they absorb all other life, and in the end no life in all these realms is fully real except insofar as, in the spiritual world, it has become human.[15]
>
> Accordingly, to the end their love of esoteric imagery confronted uneasily the hope of a sterner universality; requiring each generation to reinterpret

> for its own needs the imam that should guarantee its universal vision—the abstract history that should enshrine its truth—the sense of its intellectual mastery over the world.[16]

With the Mongol conquest, however, and the destruction of the Assassins' power, the votaries of reason were finally defeated, but those of history, too, found themselves liberated by their pagan masters from the stewardship of an empire, and it was this event that in Hodgson's view allowed the sacred law to become an autonomous and potentially universal entity.[17] Yet he held that the challenge of Ismailism's universality made for an intellectual narrowing of Sunnism, while at the same time injecting a passionately Shiʿa sense of the inner life into it by way of Sufism, which came into its own precisely after the Mongol conquest. Unlike this latter, however, Hodgson maintained that Ismailism was defined by a quest for power and universality projected into the future, something that he found cold if not inhuman, but that accorded very well with Iqbal's view of Islam, of which he was equally critical.

Hodgson understood Ismailism's antinomianism in a Pauline way, and therefore as something insufficient and even inhuman, because God had not yet become man. He claimed instead that the imam merely represented community authority and thus human agency in a merely abstract way.[18] But this made the imam play the very role that Iqbal had reserved for man, since the Ismailis, too, saw the Prophet as closing the period of sacred law as a purely external form of guidance. Or as Hodgson put it, inadvertently echoing Iqbal on the way in which the Prophet's finality gained humanity its freedom, "Despite the more bizarre aspects of the faith, fundamentally it was an attempt to express the same sort of spiritual adulthood as that of the Christianity that also threw off the yoke of the Law. That is, the time had come when artificial rules meant to curb the ignorant for his own good were no longer necessary, for the child had learned to manipulate his environment himself in full awareness of what was involved: he could allow his decisions to arise not from a contrived code or an imposed ritual of reminder, but from the spirit of the situation."[19]

Having noted the inability of the sacred law to grasp and ground the modern world spiritually, both Hodgson and Iqbal returned to its founding moment as a universal enterprise. And however secretly or disingenuously, they rescued from its ruins the esoteric language of the law's defeated rival. In other words it was no longer the law which gave Islam its universality so much as a new kind of Muslim self, whose precedents, both men realized, could only be sought in the heretical and mystical past that had ostensibly been overcome by the sharia and its focus on what Hodgson called social relations. Is this why Iqbal was unable to abandon the esoteric vocabulary of Sufism and its heretical predecessors, whose absolute dominance in his work Hodgson had noticed? And how about Hodgson's own attempt, by way of his analysis of Iqbal, to find modern Islam's universality in the mediating role of a community that, like India's Muslim minority, could no longer define social life as a whole?

Notes

1. See for this Faisal Devji, *The Impossible Indian: Gandhi and the Temptation of Violence* (Cambridge, MA: Harvard University Press, 2012), chap. 2.

2. Dipesh Chakrabarty, *Provincializing Europe: Postcolonial Thought and Historical Difference* (Princeton, NJ: Princeton University Press, 2000), 8.

3. The classic text here is M. K. Gandhi, *Hind Swaraj*, ed. A. J. Parel (Cambridge: Cambridge University Press, 1997).

4. Marshall G. S. Hodgson, *The Venture of Islam: Conscience and History in a World Civilization*, 3 vols. (Chicago: University of Chicago Press, 1974), 3:411 (hereafter cited in the text as *Venture*).

5. Marshall G. S. Hodgson, "The Role of Islam in World History," in *Rethinking World History: Essays on Europe, Islam, and World History*, ed. Edmund Burke III (Cambridge: Cambridge University Press, 2002), 97 (hereafter this volume is cited in the text as *Rethinking*).

6. See for this Carl Schmitt, *The Nomos of the Earth in the International Law of Jus Publicum Europaeum*, trans. G. L. Ulmen (New York: Telos Press, 2006).

7. For an example of his reasoning on this issue, see Muhammad Iqbal, *The Reconstruction of Religious Thought in Islam* (New Delhi: Kitab Bhavan, 1990), chap. 5.

8. See for this Faisal Devji, *Muslim Zion: Pakistan as a Political Idea* (Cambridge, MA: Harvard University Press, 2013), chap. 4.

9. Muhammad Iqbal, "Presidential Address delivered at the Annual Session of the All-India Muslim League at Allahabad on the 29th December, 1930," in *Thoughts and Reflections of Iqbal*, ed. S. A. Vahid (Lahore: Sh. Muhammad Ashraf, 1992), 161–94.

10. Muhammad Iqbal, *The Development of Metaphysics in Persia: A Contribution to the History of Muslim Philosophy* (Lahore: Bazm-i-Iqbal, 1959), 21.

11. Ibid., 38.

12. Ibid., 48.

13. Ibid., 149.

14. Ibid., 130.

15. Marshall G. S. Hodgson, *The Secret Order of Assassins* (Philadelphia: University of Pennsylvania Press, 2005), 169.

16. Ibid., 264.

17. Ibid., 271.

18. Ibid., 177.

19. Ibid., 175–76.

CONTRIBUTORS

CHRISTOPHER A. BAYLY (1945–2015) was, from 1992 to 2013, the Vere Harmsworth Professor of Imperial and Naval History at the University of Cambridge. In 2014, Bayly became the inaugural Swami Vivekananda Professor in South Asian Studies at the University of Chicago.

EDMUND BURKE III is emeritus professor of history at the University of California, Santa Cruz.

ABDESSELAM CHEDDADI is emeritus professor of history at the Université Mohammed V in Rabat.

PAMELA KYLE CROSSLEY is professor of history at Dartmouth College.

JOCELYNE DAKHLIA is director of studies at the École des hautes études en sciences sociales.

FAISAL DEVJI is University Reader in Modern South Asian History at St. Antony's College, University of Oxford.

MICHAEL GEYER is Samuel N. Harper Professor Emeritus of German and European History and in the College at the University of Chicago.

ROBERT J. MANKIN (1952–2017) was director of Anglophone studies at the Université Paris-Diderot.

KATJA NAUMANN is researcher at the Leipzig Centre for the History and Culture of East Central Europe and lecturer at the Global and European Studies Institute at the Leipzig University.